For my five grandchildren, three of whom have inherited my sour palate and just love verjuice . . . I'm working on the other two! And Sarah Goodwin, who totally gets everything about me, and verjuice too!

Maggie Beer is one of Australia's best-known cooks. In addition to co-hosting *The Cook and The Chef* and making regular appearances on *MasterChef Australia*, Maggie devotes her time to the Farmshop in the Barossa Valley where it all began, and to her export kitchen which produces her famous pate, fruit pastes, jams, sauces and verjuice, as well as a range of super-indulgent ice creams.

Maggie is the author of six successful cookbooks, *Maggie's Kitchen*, *Maggie's Harvest*, *Maggie's Table*, *Cooking with Verjuice*, *Maggie's Orchard* and *Maggie's Farm*, and co-author of the bestselling *Stephanie Alexander and Maggie Beer's Tuscan Cookbook*.

Her website is maggiebeer.com.au.

Maggie's Verjuice Cookbook

MAGGIE BEER

PHOTOGRAPHY BY
Sharyn Cairns

LANTERN
an imprint of
PENGUIN BOOKS

CONTENTS

INTRODUCTION

I can't count the number of times I've been asked, 'Just what is this verjuice you seem to love so much?'

For those of you who have never heard of it, or have bought a bottle and found that it languished at the back of the cupboard for ages while you tried to find a use for it, I thought it might be helpful to give a simple explanation of what it is and how I think it can improve your cooking.

Verjuice, literally meaning 'green juice', is the juice of unripe grapes. In cooking terms, it's what's known as an acidulant, which gives a sour flavour (often referred to as sharpness or bite) to foods. Good food always has a pleasing balance of flavours on the palate and, whether we consciously think about it or not, an acidulant is necessary to give a 'brightness' to food. Indeed, without it, flavours can be flat.

Of all acidulants, verjuice is the most gentle. It truly lifts the flavour of food without dominating, and I know of no better way to enhance flavour, no better way to make food taste fresh and alive. That doesn't mean I ignore the more common acidulants – lemon juice, vinegar or wine – all of which I use in my cooking (and all of which can be used in place of verjuice, just in lesser amounts), but I prefer the gentleness of verjuice. It is also wine-friendly, which is good to keep in mind if matching wine to food is important to you.

Verjuice has a long history, having been used in cooking for centuries throughout Europe and the Middle East. In the Middle Ages it was made from sour fruits such as gooseberries, crabapples and plums, however the practice of using unripe grapes (either those picked early to thin out the crop, or those growing too high on the bunch to ripen enough for winemaking) is the one that has endured over time. In fact, in many wine-growing countries it is still a part of the peasant farming culture to make verjuice (known as verjus in France, agresto in Italy, agraz in Spain, hosrum in Lebanon and abghooreh in Iran). It's all about the principle of wasting nothing.

This philosophy is one that I share, and which would ultimately lead me to discover verjuice myself. My husband Colin and I became vignerons and game farmers in the Barossa Valley in 1973, and six years later we opened the Farmshop, where we sold our produce (pheasant, quail, guinea fowl and grapes) prepared and cooked in different ways. Being completely untrained as a cook, I immersed myself in books on food from Mediterranean cultures. I was hungry for ideas, and reading about food was my education. First was Elizabeth David's *French Provincial Cooking*, followed by several works by female cooks from rural France who inspired me to become what I am today, a country cook who makes the most of the produce I have to hand. (Having been raised in Sydney, it's sometimes a surprise to me that I took to country living like a duck to water, and completely immersed myself in the rhythm of the seasons in this beautiful valley.) I positively devoured these books, and it was through them that I learnt about verjuice for the first time. They piqued my interest – just reading about verjuice I felt a sense of affinity with it, almost as if I could 'taste' it as I read. Given my preference for sour flavours, I just knew it was going to be something I would love.

Life is all about timing. In 1984, we couldn't sell our crop of rhine riesling grapes, so I convinced a great friend of mine, winemaker Peter Wall, to help me make verjuice. In a classic case of necessity being the mother of invention, we forged ahead, without a recipe, a method or even a benchmark to work towards. What a beginning it was! I was so proud of my flagons of verjuice that I sat them above the mantelpiece of the fire at the restaurant . . . and shouldn't have been surprised when they exploded!

In those early days I gave my verjuice to chefs I knew and admired, including Stephanie Alexander, Janni Kyritsis and Lew Kathreptis, and began to use it myself. From such humble beginnings, I never dreamt of the huge journey it would take me on. I'm told that I was the first in the world to make verjuice on a commercial scale. What delights me more is that it is now being produced commercially in many countries across the world – which, to me, legitimises it as a staple ingredient in the kitchen.

Much has changed since those early days. As well as the classic verjuice, we now produce a slightly sweeter version, the beautifully pink-hued Sangiovese verjuice, made from crushed red grapes. I find this is a perfect companion to desserts, though it works in savoury dishes too (and it's pretty special in a gin and tonic!). Interestingly, it's a little known fact that verjuice can be enjoyed as a drink; over the years, I've had many a refreshing glass of verjuice with ice and fresh mint to cool me down whilst toiling in a hot kitchen. I've even had cocktails made with verjuice named after me – great fun! While too sour for some people, funnily enough three of my five grand-children – Ben, Rory and Zoe – absolutely love to drink verjuice. In fact, from when he could first talk, Ben has been asking for a glass of 'white' or 'pink' whenever he visits the Farmshop. My love of drinking verjuice led me to develop another drink based on the unfermented juice of grapes, Sparkling Ruby Cabernet. This is made from early harvest grapes, though it's not as sour as verjuice, but fruity and tart instead.

I hope that you can see from this collection of over 100 recipes that you can use verjuice in all your cooking – it's not just for salad dressings. Try it in everything from soups and braises, seafood dishes, pasta and grills to delicate desserts and hearty puds (I feel the list is endless . . .). Some of the recipes in this book use verjuice as a key flavour, whereas others use the lightest drizzle right at the end to lift the dish to another level.

One of the easiest, and I think best, ways to use verjuice is to add it to a pan of hot roasted vegetables towards the end of cooking, using a basic technique called deglazing. This transforms ordinary roasted veg into something really special, giving them a brightness of flavour and a syrupy sheen that is irresistible. Served on bruschetta (see recipe on page 28), these are a real hit at our daily cooking demonstrations at the Farmshop, where visitors can learn a few simple ways to cook with verjuice and taste the spoils. Even in the depths of winter, I'm always amazed at how people appear from nowhere, just around lunchtime, to take in the heady smells and sample some of our fare. I'm no longer surprised when they linger afterwards to ask questions of my team about verjuice, and I love being able to share my experience of this extraordinary ingredient with so many people.

I encourage you to try cooking with verjuice – it's such a simple way to add flavour to your food. Try it in one or two recipes to start with, and soon you might find yourself adding a splash here, and a splash there, to liven up all kinds of dishes. You might even, in the words of my fabulous recipe tester for this book, Fiona Hammond, find yourself becoming a verjuice junkie! I hope these recipes inspire you to find your own way to add a bit of magic to your cooking.

If you have a grapevine in your garden, you can even make your own verjuice. All you need to do is pick the grapes when they are just beginning to swell a little, but are still very tart. Crush them in a mouli or push them through a fine-meshed sieve, discarding the skins and seeds, and then pour the juice into ice-cube trays and freeze. When you need the beautiful piquancy of verjuice, simply throw a cube or two into whatever you're cooking.

BEGINNING

Black Olives with Walnuts and Orange Zest

This dish is a variation on a favourite theme of mine, that of matching olives with nuts and citrus zest. In the past I've used green olives, but the flavour of mature black olives works equally well. The main thing here is that it offers a way of serving olives that's different to what's available ready-made in the shops. You can do your own thing when it comes to flavourings (using the best-quality ingredients), then serve the olives warm for a really special treat.

SERVES 10 FOR NIBBLES

120 g walnuts
2½ cups (300 g) black olives
100 ml verjuice
zest of 1 orange, removed in thin strips with a vegetable peeler, leaving the bitter pith
3 sprigs rosemary
6 bay leaves
½ cup (125 ml) extra virgin olive oil

Preheat a fan-forced oven to 200°C (220°C).

Place the walnuts on a baking tray and roast for 5 minutes or until golden, checking them frequently to make sure they don't burn. Immediately wrap in a clean tea towel and rub to peel off the skins. Shake the walnuts in a sieve to get rid of the skins, then set aside to cool.

Place the olives, verjuice, orange zest, rosemary, bay leaves and 100 ml water in a small baking dish. Press a sheet of baking paper down onto the olive mixture and cover the dish tightly with foil. Transfer to the oven to braise for 1 hour, checking after 40 minutes that the liquid hasn't evaporated (add ¼ cup [60 ml] water if so). After an hour, remove the dish from the oven and leave the olives to cool for 10 minutes in the juices.

Drain the olive mixture and discard the rosemary, then toss with the roasted walnuts and olive oil. Transfer to a bowl and serve warm.

Scallops with Preserved Lemon and Caper Butter

We're very lucky to have access to so many wonderful varieties of scallop in Australia. The quality of Port Lincoln scallops is well established, and I've heard my friend Cheong Liew wax lyrical about Rottnest Island scallops. Recently I ate a wonderful queen scallop on a ferry ride from Bruny Island in Tasmania. It was one of the largest scallops I'd seen and, when fresh, so sweet to eat raw. There is a huge difference, however, between fresh scallops and those that have been frozen. Frozen scallops release moisture when they cook, so they're more likely to poach than fry. Sadly, you sometimes see frozen scallops sold as fresh, so try to buy from a fishmonger who can vouch for the freshness of the catch. The preserved lemon and caper butter here is a great accompaniment, but a touch of sea salt and freshly ground black pepper works just as well – as long as you first cook the scallops in plenty of nut-brown butter.

SERVES 4 AS AN ENTREE

---

12 scallops on the half-shell, roe intact
finely grated zest of 1 lime
1 tablespoon extra virgin olive oil, plus extra for drizzling
sea salt and freshly ground black pepper
80 g unsalted butter
⅓ cup (80 ml) verjuice
chervil leaves, to serve

PRESERVED LEMON AND CAPER BUTTER

1 quarter preserved lemon, flesh removed and rind rinsed
100 g unsalted butter, softened and chopped
1 teaspoon salted capers, rinsed
1 tablespoon verjuice
1 tablespoon chervil leaves

To make the preserved lemon and caper butter, place all the ingredients in a food processor and process until well combined. Transfer the flavoured butter to a sheet of plastic film and roll into a 3 cm thick log, then wrap in baking paper and chill in the refrigerator for at least 30 minutes to firm up or until ready to use.

Meanwhile, to clean the scallops, pull the meat away from the shell, then cut out and discard the dark intestinal tract, keeping the roe intact. Wash and dry the shells, then spread out in a single layer on a baking tray.

Toss the scallops with the lime zest and oil in a bowl, then season with salt and pepper.

Preheat a fan-forced oven to 180°C (200°C).

Melt half of the butter in a frying pan over high heat until sizzling, then add a splash of extra oil to stop the butter burning. Add six of the scallops and cook on one side for 30 seconds or until golden around the edges, then turn and cook for a further 30 seconds. Add half of the verjuice and cook, stirring, for 1 minute or until it has evaporated. Place each scallop in a clean, dry scallop shell. Wipe out the pan with paper towel and quickly repeat the process with the remaining butter, scallops and verjuice.

Top each scallop with a generous slice of the preserved lemon and caper butter and place the tray in the oven for 1 minute or just until the butter begins to melt.

Top each scallop with a chervil leaf and serve at once.

JELLIES MADE WITH VERJUICE Simple as these are, these jellies are something I never tire of. There is something quite magical about the sight of perfectly ripe cubes of avocado, mushrooms of varying shapes and sizes or generous chunks of smoked ocean trout suspended in a verjuice and French tarragon jelly. I usually make them in 'recycled' 125 ml pate moulds to serve as a wonderfully refreshing starter or, if serving them at a cocktail party, I use Chinese soup spoons. French tarragon is only available in spring and summer but you could substitute chervil at other times of the year.

PICTURED OVERLEAF > LEFT: Avocado Jelly CENTRE: Mushroom Jelly RIGHT: Smoked Ocean Trout Jelly

Mushroom Jellies

MAKES 6

1½ cups (375 ml) verjuice
2 sprigs French tarragon
1 teaspoon caster sugar
2½ x 2 g gold-strength gelatine leaves
40 g unsalted butter, plus extra if needed
1 tablespoon extra virgin olive oil
130 g small Swiss brown mushrooms, thinly sliced
sea salt
150 g small abalone mushrooms, bases trimmed
200 g enoki mushrooms, trimmed (you need 150 g after trimming)
extra virgin olive oil and micro herbs (optional), to serve

Place the verjuice, tarragon sprigs and sugar in a small stainless-steel saucepan over low–medium heat, then bring just to a simmer, being careful not to let it boil or the verjuice will become cloudy. Remove from the heat and set aside to infuse for 10 minutes.

Soak the gelatine leaves in a small bowl of cold water for 5 minutes until softened. Remove the gelatine and squeeze out any excess liquid. Add to the warm verjuice and stir until the gelatine has dissolved. Remove the tarragon and discard. Set aside to cool to room temperature.

Melt the butter in a large frying pan over medium heat and cook until nut-brown, adding the olive oil when the butter starts to bubble to prevent it from burning. Add the Swiss brown mushrooms, season with salt and quickly toss for 2 minutes until just softened, then transfer to a plate lined with paper towel. Add the abalone mushrooms to the pan, adding a little extra butter if needed, then cook for 2 minutes until softened and transfer to the paper-towel-lined plate. Add the enoki mushrooms to the pan, adding a little extra butter if needed, then toss for 1–2 minutes until just softened. Transfer to the paper-towel-lined plate.

Have ready six 125 ml moulds. Divide the enoki mushrooms among the moulds, swirling so the mushrooms coat the side of each mould (they will adhere quite easily). Divide the abalone mushrooms around the edge of each mould, then fill the centre of each mould with one-sixth of the Swiss brown mushrooms. Carefully divide the verjuice mixture among the moulds. Cover each mould with plastic film, pressing it lightly down onto the surface.

Refrigerate the jellies for 4 hours or until set.

To turn the jellies out of the moulds, dip the base of each mould in a bowl of hot water for 30 seconds, then invert the jelly onto a serving plate. Drizzle with olive oil and scatter with micro herbs, if using, before serving.

Avocado Jellies

MAKES 6

1½ cups (375 ml) verjuice
2 sprigs French tarragon,
plus 18 extra leaves for moulds
1 teaspoon caster sugar
2½ × 2 g gold-strength gelatine leaves
2 large ripe avocados
squeeze of lemon juice
sea salt
extra virgin olive oil and chervil sprigs or
micro herbs (optional), to serve

Place the verjuice, tarragon sprigs and sugar in a small stainless-steel saucepan over low–medium heat, then bring just to a simmer, being careful not to let it boil or the verjuice will become cloudy. Remove from the heat and set aside to infuse for 10 minutes.

Soak the gelatine leaves in a small bowl of cold water for 5 minutes until softened. Remove the gelatine and squeeze out any excess liquid. Add to the warm verjuice and stir until the gelatine has dissolved. Remove the tarragon and discard. Set aside to cool to room temperature.

Cut the avocados into 5 mm dice and squeeze with a little lemon juice to stop them discolouring.

Have ready six 125 ml moulds. Place three tarragon leaves in the base of each mould and distribute the avocado evenly among the moulds. Carefully divide the verjuice mixture among the moulds. Cover each mould with plastic film, pressing it lightly down onto the surface.

Refrigerate the jellies for 4 hours or until set.

To turn the jellies out of the moulds, dip the base of each mould in a bowl of hot water for 30 seconds, then invert the jelly onto a serving plate. Season with salt, drizzle with olive oil and scatter with micro herbs, if using, before serving.

Smoked Ocean Trout Jellies

MAKES 6

1½ cups (375 ml) verjuice
3 sprigs French tarragon
1 teaspoon caster sugar
2½ × 2 g gold-strength gelatine leaves
handful snipped chives
350 g lightly smoked ocean trout, skin and bones
removed, flesh broken into small chunks
sea salt
extra virgin olive oil and chervil sprigs or
micro herbs (optional), to serve

Place the verjuice, tarragon sprigs and sugar in a small stainless-steel saucepan over low–medium heat, then bring just to a simmer, being careful not to let it boil or the verjuice will become cloudy. Remove from the heat and set aside to infuse for 10 minutes.

Soak the gelatine leaves in a small bowl of cold water for 5 minutes until softened. Remove the gelatine and squeeze out any excess liquid. Add to the warm verjuice and stir until the gelatine has dissolved. Remove the tarragon and discard. Set aside to cool to room temperature.

Have ready six 125 ml moulds. Scatter some chives into the base of each mould, then distribute the smoked trout evenly among the moulds. Carefully divide the verjuice mixture among the moulds. Cover each mould with plastic film, pressing it lightly down onto the surface.

Refrigerate the jellies for 4 hours or until set.

To turn the jellies out of the moulds, dip the base of each mould in a bowl of hot water for 30 seconds, then invert the jelly onto a serving plate. Season with salt, drizzle with olive oil and scatter with micro herbs, if using, before serving.

Devils on Horseback

These – and angels on horseback (oysters wrapped in bacon) – are firm favourites with my grandchildren. It's not just because of the great bacon I use (my daughter Saskia's Black Pig traditionally smoked belly bacon, with its sweet fat I rave about), it's the sweet/salty and sweet/sour combinations that work so well. These could well be called old-fashioned food, but for me there's no such thing as fashion in food – all that counts is flavour. Just try these next time you have friends around and see how well they go. While I've cooked them on the barbecue, you could also pop them under the grill: preheat to medium–high and place them about 5 cm from the heat. Cook for 3–4 minutes, turning to cook evenly on all sides, until brown and crisp. Also, make sure the bacon you use is thin enough and long enough to wrap right around the prune, then use a toothpick to keep in place.

MAKES 24

---

1 tablespoon extra virgin olive oil
1 sprig rosemary
⅓ cup (80 ml) verjuice
zest and juice of 1 small orange, zest removed in thin strips with a vegetable peeler, leaving the bitter pith
24 prunes, pitted
24 very thin rashers traditionally smoked belly bacon
sea salt

Place the oil and rosemary in a small frying pan over low–medium heat and fry for 1 minute or until aromatic. Add the verjuice, zest and orange juice, then increase the heat to high and simmer for 3 minutes. Reduce the heat to low and toss in the prunes, then simmer for 3 minutes. Remove the pan from the heat and set aside for 45 minutes or until cooled to room temperature, then drain.

Cut the orange zest strips into 24 small pieces. Place a piece on each prune, then wrap with a rasher of bacon and secure with a toothpick.

Cook on a hot barbecue grill plate for 2 minutes on one side until browned, taking care that they don't burn, then turn and cook for 1 minute on the other side or until the bacon is dark golden-brown and crisp. Season with a little salt and serve immediately.

Artichokes with Verjuice Hollandaise

This is the simplest way to cook artichokes without any of the usual preparation. While the flour in the water isn't essential, it does keep the outer leaves of the artichoke from going more grey than green. Even though you end up taking off all those outer leaves as you eat the artichoke, I think this first impression is important (we do eat with our eyes, as they say). I will be bold here and say that the flavour of the verjuice hollandaise is beyond measure; so wonderfully sweet and nutty, it's totally addictive. If you don't like the pressure of making a sauce that needs to be served warm at the last moment, buy yourself a wide-necked thermos flask that will keep it warm without spoiling. I can assure you it won't go to waste, as you'll find lots of other reasons for making this sauce . . . just try it with fresh asparagus!

SERVES 2–4 AS AN ENTREE

⅓ cup (50 g) plain flour
1 cup (250 ml) verjuice *or* 2 lemons, sliced
sea salt
4 globe artichokes, stalks trimmed, leaving 3 cm intact

VERJUICE HOLLANDAISE
1 cup (250 ml) verjuice
1 bay leaf
6 black peppercorns
250 g unsalted butter, chopped
4 egg yolks
sea salt and freshly ground white pepper

Add water to a large stainless-steel saucepan until it is two-thirds full and whisk in the flour. Place the pan over high heat, then add the verjuice or lemon slices and 1 teaspoon salt and bring to the boil. Add the artichokes, then weigh them down with a small plate to immerse them. Reduce the heat to medium and bring back to a simmer, then cook for 20–25 minutes or until the artichokes are tender when a knife or skewer is inserted into the centre.

Meanwhile, to make the hollandaise, place the verjuice, bay leaf and peppercorns in a small stainless-steel saucepan over high heat. Bring to the boil and simmer for 9 minutes or until reduced to 2 tablespoons. Strain and set aside to cool.

Melt the butter in a small saucepan over high heat and cook for 5–6 minutes or until nut-brown, then remove from the heat. Pour the butter into a jug, leaving any residual brown solids behind in the saucepan. Set aside to cool for 10–12 minutes (if you have a digital thermometer, the temperature should register 69°C).

Place the egg yolks and cooled verjuice mixture in a small food processor and process to emulsify. With the motor running, add the nut-brown butter a little at a time until fully incorporated. Check the sauce for seasoning and add salt and pepper, if desired.

Carefully remove the artichokes from the pan and stand stalk-side up in a colander to drain excess water. When cool enough to handle, trim the base of the stems and remove a few leaves from the bottom. Carefully open up the artichokes like a flower and scrape out the hairy choke with a teaspoon.

Serve immediately, with warm verjuice hollandaise alongside for dipping.

Kingfish Sashimi with Avocado and Wasabi Cream

Hiramasa kingfish from South Australia is a truly great farmed fish – aquaculture at its best, I think. Very fresh kingfish, carved and served as sashimi, is a great favourite in our family. I have to admit I love to eat kingfish raw (I'm happy as Larry to have nothing more with it than extra virgin olive oil and salt), but Colin prefers an acidulant with his to 'cook' the fish. Whether you trim the bloodline or not when carving the kingfish comes down to personal preference; some feel that showing the bloodline confirms the freshness of the fish. You can ask your fishmonger to remove it if you're not confident doing it yourself. If carving the fish more than 5 minutes in advance of serving, be sure to cover it tightly with plastic film to prevent oxidisation. The avocado and wasabi cream is a luscious accompaniment. It's funny how I can't eat chilli, yet I love horseradish and wasabi . . .

SERVES 8 AS AN ENTREE

2 small golden shallots, finely chopped
½ cup (125 ml) verjuice
¼ cup (60 ml) extra virgin olive oil
sea salt and freshly ground black pepper
1 × 400 g kingfish fillet, skin-on, trimmed of bloodline, if desired
mache (lambs' lettuce) leaves, to garnish
lemon wedges (optional), to serve

AVOCADO AND WASABI CREAM
1 large ripe avocado
1 teaspoon verjuice
1 teaspoon wasabi paste (or more to taste)
¼ cup (60 ml) Verjuice Mayonnaise (see page 193)
1 tablespoon chopped chervil (optional)

Place the shallot and verjuice in a small stainless-steel saucepan over high heat. Bring to the boil and simmer for 6 minutes or until reduced to 2 tablespoons. Remove from the heat and stir in the olive oil, then season to taste with salt and pepper. Set aside for 15 minutes or until cooled to room temperature.

Holding on to the skin, thinly slice the kingfish with a sharp flexible knife. Overlap the slices on a serving dish. Discard the skin.

To make the avocado and wasabi cream, scoop the avocado flesh into a bowl and mash with the back of a fork (you could use a food processor if the avocado is not very ripe). Drizzle over the verjuice, then mix in a little of the wasabi paste, tasting and adding more as desired. Stir in the mayonnaise until well combined, then add the chervil, if using. Taste and adjust the seasoning if necessary.

Drizzle the cooled shallot mixture over the kingfish and garnish with mache leaves, if using. Serve with spoonfuls of the avocado and wasabi cream to the side and some lemon wedges, if you like.

Grilled Vegetables with Verjuice and Extra Virgin Olive Oil

We tend to eat outside most weeknights in summer and autumn. Grilling meat and vegetables such as these on the barbecue and serving them with a freshly picked garden salad is the normal order of the day. No matter how rushed the day has been, life is definitely too short not to take the time to enjoy good food every day. This can be as simple as making the most of what is in season, and these grilled vegetables rested in a bath of extra virgin olive oil and verjuice are a perfect example. All the vegetables can be cooked on the barbecue grill plate following the order I've given here, so they are ready at the same time.

SERVES 4 AS AN ACCOMPANIMENT

---

2 small red onions, halved crossways
2 bulbs baby fennel, trimmed, halved lengthways *or* 1 large bulb cut lengthways into 1.5 cm thick slices, fronds reserved to garnish
2 small or 1 large red capsicum (pepper), halved lengthways (if large, cut into quarters), white membrane and seeds removed
2 Japanese eggplants (aubergines), sliced lengthways, flesh scored
2 small zucchini (courgettes), halved lengthways
⅔ cup (160 ml) extra virgin olive oil
sea salt

POST-COOKING MARINADE
⅔ cup (160 ml) extra virgin olive oil
⅔ cup (160 ml) verjuice
1 lemon (preferably a meyer lemon), cut in half and thinly sliced
small handful roughly chopped flat-leaf parsley leaves

Preheat a barbecue grill plate to high.

Place the onion, fennel, capsicum, eggplant and zucchini in a large roasting pan or mixing bowl, then add the olive oil and toss to coat well. Season with salt.

Place the onion, cut-side down, on the barbecue and grill for 15–20 minutes. After 5 minutes, add the fennel and cook for 10–15 minutes, then add the eggplant and cook for 10–12 minutes. Add the capsicum and cook for 8 minutes or until the skin blackens and blisters, then remove from the barbecue and peel off the skin. Finally, add the zucchini and cook for 6–8 minutes: turn over all except the onion halfway through the cooking.

Meanwhile, to make the post-cooking marinade, whisk the oil and verjuice together in a large shallow dish, then add the lemon and parsley and set aside.

Remove the vegetables from the grill plate as they are ready and place them in the post-cooking marinade. Set aside until ready to serve.

To serve, transfer the warm vegetables to a platter, drizzle with some of the marinade and garnish with the lemon slices, parsley and fennel fronds.

Garfish with Pistou in Vine Leaves

The idea of cooking food wrapped in leaves is age-old, and I take my lead with this from the Italian culture, here using fish. You could use any type of small fish for this: southern herring and whiting are both wonderful, but would need to be cooked slightly longer. I blanch my own vine leaves in verjuice (which, given we have a large vineyard, is only common sense), but you could use bought preserved vine leaves and soak them well beforehand to rid them of excess salt. Cooking the fish parcels on a charcoal-fuelled kettle barbecue adds another dimension of flavour and is a more gentle way of cooking. Just make sure you provide finger bowls for your guests!

SERVES 4 AS A LIGHT MEAL

8 large fresh vine leaves
8 garfish (about 80 g each), cleaned and scaled
extra virgin olive oil, for brushing and drizzling
sea salt
2 tablespoons verjuice
lemon wedges, to serve

PISTOU

2 handfuls flat-leaf parsley leaves
2 handfuls marjoram leaves
1 tablespoon chopped preserved lemon rind, rinsed
¼ cup (60 ml) extra virgin olive oil
2 tablespoons verjuice

To make the pistou, place the parsley, marjoram and preserved lemon in a food processor and blend for 1 minute, slowly pouring in the oil while the motor is running; you may need to stop and scrape down the side of the bowl with a flexible spatula now and then. With the motor running, add the verjuice and blend for 1 minute or until a paste has formed, then set aside.

Preheat a barbecue grill plate to high.

Plunge the vine leaves into a saucepan of boiling water for 1 minute. Rinse under cold water, drain well and spread out in a single layer to cool.

Spread the centre of each leaf with a little pistou. Place a garfish on top, then wrap the leaf around the fish. Lightly brush with olive oil and sprinkle with salt.

Place the garfish on the hot grill plate and cook for 2 minutes, then turn and cook for a further 1½ minutes. Transfer to a plate to rest for a few minutes, then drizzle with verjuice and oil. Serve with wedges of lemon.

Baked Mushrooms with Gruth >

Gruth, which takes its name from an old Gaelic word for curd, is a fresh cheese made by Ballycroft Artisan Cheese in the Barossa. They first warm soured milk and then use a traditional method of hanging the curds in muslin to drain. It's a cheese I love to use in so many ways as its slight acidity balances well with its creaminess – use quark or top-quality ricotta if you can't get hold of gruth. Turn this into a delicious light meal by serving the mushrooms on bruschetta: grill thick slices of ciabatta then rub them all over with a cut clove of garlic. Drizzle over some extra virgin olive oil and season with salt, then place a mushroom on top and finish with a dollop of gruth. Return this to the oven for 3–4 minutes, then serve with a final flourish of oil and some chopped flat-leaf parsley.

SERVES 6 AS AN ACCOMPANIMENT

- 6 very large flat field mushrooms, stalks removed
- ⅓ cup (80 ml) extra virgin olive oil
- 6 sprigs thyme
- sea salt
- ¼ cup (60 ml) verjuice
- 300 g gruth, quark or ricotta

Preheat a fan-forced oven to 200°C (220°C).

Choose a baking dish just large enough to hold the mushrooms in one layer, then cover the base with ¼ cup (60 ml) of the oil. Place the mushrooms in the dish, then top each one with a thyme sprig and sprinkle with salt. Drizzle the remaining oil evenly over the mushrooms.

Bake the mushrooms for 35–40 minutes or until tender. Pour the verjuice over and bake for a further 5 minutes.

Serve the mushrooms with the gruth alongside.

Salmon with Verjuice Citrus Dressing

Salmon has become a convenience food in our household, and raw is our favourite way of eating it. Living in the Barossa, I don't often get to a fish market, however I can get a fresh side of salmon delivered, which I cut into portion sizes, wrap in plastic film and freeze flat on a tray (salmon is pretty much the only fish I would freeze – it fares well due to its fat content). If thawed out slowly in the refrigerator so the moisture dissipates, it can be carved so close to fresh it's surprising. The dressing makes more than you'll need here, but the leftovers can be used to dress a shredded chicken salad or to drizzle over steamed vegetables.

SERVES 4

- 1 × 280 g piece sashimi-grade salmon

VERJUICE CITRUS DRESSING

- 1 tablespoon finely grated lemon zest
- 2 teaspoons finely grated orange zest
- 1 small clove garlic, finely chopped
- small handful roughly chopped flat-leaf parsley
- 1 teaspoon finely chopped mint
- 2 teaspoons finely chopped chervil
- ¼ cup (60 ml) verjuice
- sea salt
- ½ cup (125 ml) extra virgin olive oil

To make the dressing, place the citrus zests, garlic, herbs, verjuice and ¼ teaspoon salt in a small food processor and combine. With the motor running, gradually drizzle in the olive oil in a steady stream until incorporated. Transfer to a screw-top jar with a lid and set aside for 1 hour to allow the flavours to infuse.

Thinly slice the salmon across the grain and divide among four serving plates. Shake the dressing in the jar to combine then drizzle over the salmon to taste.

Cockles with Chorizo

I had always believed that if a mussel, cockle or clam did not open during cooking then it should be thrown away, but recently an article by Dr Karl Kruszelnicki in the *Sydney Morning Herald*'s *Good Weekend* magazine put me right. He explained that you can prise the stubborn ones open, and as long as they don't smell off, they're fine to use. The important thing here is not to overcook the cockles or they will shrink and become rubbery. The same applies when frying the chorizo: you're really just warming it through, to give the dish a fabulous smoky flavour.

SERVES 2 AS AN ENTREE

1 kg South Australian cockles (pipis) or clams
1 cup (250 ml) Fish Stock (see page 191)
1½ tablespoons extra virgin olive oil
150 g chorizo, cut in half lengthways then sliced crossways into 5 mm thick slices
sea salt and freshly ground black pepper
½ cup (125 ml) verjuice
2 tablespoons finely chopped chives
extra virgin olive oil and crusty bread, to serve

Discard any cockles with broken shells, then place the remainder in a large bowl of cold water and soak for 30 minutes to flush out any sand. Remove the cockles from the water with a slotted spoon, leaving any sand in the base of the bowl, then place in a sieve to drain.

Heat the fish stock in a small saucepan over medium heat for 2–3 minutes or until just warmed through.

Meanwhile, heat the oil in a large non-stick frying pan over high heat and fry the chorizo for 1 minute, then turn to cook the other side for 30 seconds (cook it just long enough for it to colour and release some of its oil). Transfer the chorizo to a plate, leaving the oil in the pan.

Return the pan to high heat, then add the drained cockles and toss well for 1 minute, shaking the pan to allow the oil to coat the cockles. Season with salt and pepper, then add the verjuice and cook, stirring, until it has evaporated. Add the warm fish stock, then cover and cook the cockles for 2 minutes or until they start to open. Return the chorizo to the pan and stir to combine.

Divide the cockle and chorizo mixture between two warm bowls. Sprinkle with chopped chives and splash generously with oil, then serve immediately with crusty bread to soak up the juices.

A TRIO OF BRUSCHETTA These are a star attraction at our daily cooking demonstration at the Farmshop, where visitors can learn about a few simple ways to use verjuice and taste the spoils. Instead of serving these roast veg on bruschetta, you could turn them into a more substantial meal by tossing them through freshly cooked pasta with a generous amount of Parmigiano, stirring them through a risotto or using them as a topping for homemade pizzas.

PICTURED OPPOSITE > LEFT: Mushroom Bruschetta CENTRE: Roast Pumpkin Bruschetta (see recipe overleaf) RIGHT: Roast Fennel Bruschetta

Mushroom Bruschetta

MAKES ENOUGH FOR 4 BRUSCHETTA

- 40 g unsalted butter
- 1 tablespoon extra virgin olive oil, plus extra for drizzling
- 200 g Swiss brown mushrooms, sliced
- sea salt and freshly ground black pepper
- 3 sprigs lemon thyme, leaves picked
- 2 tablespoons verjuice
- 4 thick slices ciabatta
- 1 clove garlic, cut in half
- chopped flat-leaf parsley, to serve

Melt the butter in a large frying pan over medium–high heat and cook for 2–3 minutes or until nut-brown, adding the oil when the butter starts to bubble to prevent it from burning. Add the mushrooms and stir to coat well in the butter mixture. Season with salt and pepper and throw in the lemon thyme. Reduce the heat to medium and cook for 5 minutes or until the mushrooms are cooked through, stirring occasionally.

Increase the heat to high, pour in the verjuice and cook, stirring, for 30 seconds or until the liquid has reduced by half, then remove from the heat and set aside.

Toast the ciabatta on both sides under a preheated grill, then rub all over with the cut garlic clove, drizzle with olive oil and sprinkle with salt. Top with the mushrooms, a final drizzle of oil and the parsley.

Roast Fennel Bruschetta

MAKES ENOUGH FOR 4 BRUSCHETTA

- 325 g fennel (about ½ large bulb), trimmed and cut into thin slices
- 2 tablespoons extra virgin olive oil, plus extra for drizzling
- sea salt and freshly ground black pepper
- 2 tablespoons verjuice
- 4 thick slices ciabatta
- 1 clove garlic, cut in half
- finely chopped flat-leaf parsley, to serve

Preheat a fan-forced oven to 240°C (240°C) and line a baking tray with baking paper.

In a bowl, toss the fennel slices with the oil, a pinch of salt and pepper to coat, then spread them out on the prepared baking tray and roast for 10 minutes or until golden brown and tender.

Remove the tray from the oven and drizzle the verjuice over the fennel. Roast for a further 3–5 minutes or until no liquid remains, then set aside.

Toast the ciabatta on both sides under a preheated grill, then rub all over with the cut garlic clove, drizzle with olive oil and sprinkle with salt. Top with the roast fennel, a final drizzle of oil and the parsley.

Roast Pumpkin Bruschetta

MAKES ENOUGH FOR 2 BRUSCHETTA

200 g really ripe pumpkin, peeled, seeded and cut into bite-sized pieces
2 tablespoons extra virgin olive oil, plus extra for drizzling
1 sprig rosemary, leaves picked
sea salt and freshly ground black pepper
¼ cup (60 ml) verjuice
2 thick slices ciabatta
1 clove garlic, cut in half
soft goat's curd, to serve

Preheat a fan-forced oven to 240°C (240°C) and line a baking tray with baking paper.

Place the pumpkin, olive oil, rosemary and some salt and pepper in a bowl and toss to coat the pumpkin, then spread on a baking tray and roast for 20–25 minutes or until cooked and coloured but still firm.

Remove the tray from the oven and drizzle the verjuice over the pumpkin. Roast for a further 3–5 minutes or until no liquid remains, then set aside.

Toast the ciabatta on both sides under a preheated grill, then rub all over with the cut garlic clove and drizzle with olive oil. Spread with a thick layer of goat's curd, top with the pumpkin and rosemary and finish with a final sprinkling of salt.

Freekeh Salad

This is a salad we make every day at the Farmshop. Freekeh, an ancient grain, is a roasted green wheat that has a great nutty flavour. The brand I use, Greenwheat Freekeh, is produced on the plains outside Adelaide, and I've been a champion of it for a long time. I particularly love that it is such a great vehicle for quince paste, preserved lemons and extra virgin olive oil. The freekeh can be cooked in advance, cooled and then stored in the fridge until ready to use. The salad is best eaten on the day it is made though, as this is when the flavours will be at their best.

SERVES 6–8

180 g freekeh
sea salt
small handful roughly chopped flat-leaf parsley
small handful roughly chopped mint
4 quarters preserved lemon, flesh removed, rind rinsed and roughly chopped
75 g quince paste, cut into small dice
¼ cup (60 ml) extra virgin olive oil
1 tablespoon lemon juice
2 tablespoons verjuice

Place the freekeh into a saucepan with 2 cups (500 ml) water and 2 teaspoons salt and bring to the boil over high heat. Reduce the heat to low and cook for 20–25 minutes, stirring frequently, or until the water has been absorbed. Transfer the cooked freekeh to a tray or large plate and spread out to cool to room temperature.

Combine the cooled freekeh with the remaining ingredients in a bowl and mix well. Set aside for 1 hour before serving to allow the flavours to infuse.

Preserved Lemon and Green Bean Salad

This salad is a great accompaniment to almost any lamb, fish or chicken dish (I especially like it with the Tarragon Chicken Breasts with Grapes on page 120). Rather than discarding the flesh of the preserved lemon (as usually only the rind is used in cooking), I return it to the jar and then use it to flavour lamb shanks or other slow-cooked dishes, or I rub it over a roasted chicken. 'Nothing wasted' is my motto!

SERVES 4–6

---

2 quarters preserved lemon, flesh removed, rind rinsed and finely sliced
¼ cup (60 ml) verjuice, plus 1 tablespoon extra for soaking
½ cup (125 ml) extra virgin olive oil
1 red onion, cut into quarters
1 tablespoon vino cotto
500 g green beans, topped and tailed
freshly ground black pepper
small handful basil leaves, torn

In a small bowl, soak the preserved lemon in the extra verjuice for 30 minutes.

Heat 2 tablespoons of the oil in a small frying pan over low–medium heat. Add the onion and cook, covered, for 10 minutes or until the onion is just cooked through, turning after 5 minutes. Increase the heat to high, then add the vino cotto and cook for 1 minute, tossing to coat until the onion is a dark golden-brown. Remove from the pan and set aside to cool, removing the skins if desired.

Cook the green beans in a saucepan of boiling salted water for 3 minutes, then drain and spread the beans out on paper towel to cool quickly.

Whisk the ¼ cup (60 ml) verjuice and the remaining oil together in a bowl. Add the drained preserved lemon, the green beans and onion and toss gently to combine. Season with pepper to taste and leave for 10 minutes to allow the flavours to infuse.

Toss the basil leaves through and serve immediately.

Tomato, Saffron and Verjuice Soup with Prawns and Chervil

This soup is very quick to make and could be eaten, sans prawns, with just a flourish of extra virgin olive oil, croutons and chopped chervil. Here I've added just-cooked prawns to make it a little more special; you could also use pan-fried scallops, cooked salmon or ocean trout. It also makes a lovely chilled soup on a hot summer's day, served with some yoghurt and crusty bread.

SERVES 4

- 1 tablespoon extra virgin olive oil, plus extra for drizzling
- 1 onion, roughly chopped
- 1 clove garlic, roughly chopped
- 800 g ripe tomatoes, roughly chopped
- ⅔ cup (160 ml) verjuice
- 1½ teaspoons caster sugar
- 15 threads saffron
- sea salt
- 40 g unsalted butter
- 12 large raw prawns, peeled and deveined but with tails intact
- handful chervil sprigs

Heat the oil in a large heavy-based saucepan over medium heat. Add the onion and cook for 5 minutes, stirring occasionally, until softened. Reduce the heat to low–medium and add the garlic, then cook for a further 3–5 minutes or until the garlic is light golden-brown.

Add the tomato and increase the heat to high. Add ½ cup (125 ml) of the verjuice and cook for 2 minutes, then add the sugar, saffron, ½ teaspoon salt and 475 ml water. Bring to the boil, then reduce the heat to low–medium and simmer for 20 minutes or until the liquid has reduced by a third.

Remove the pan from the heat and blend the mixture with a stick blender until smooth. Check the seasoning and adjust as required. Cover to keep warm and set aside.

Heat the butter in a large frying pan over high heat until foaming, then add the prawns and a pinch of salt. Cook the prawns for 1 minute, then turn and cook for a further 30–40 seconds. Add the remaining verjuice and stir for 45 seconds–1 minute or until the verjuice has evaporated.

Divide the soup among four bowls, then arrange three prawns in each. Sprinkle over some chervil and finish with some of the butter from the frying pan and a splash of extra virgin olive oil before serving.

Lentil Salad with Celery Leaves

I used to be of the school of thought that eating lentils was, dare I say it, almost a punishment. Then I found I could get fresh, locally grown organic lentils from Nolans Road on South Australia's Limestone Coast. They produce both puy-style lentils and the larger, more robust green lentils (they call this variety 'Matilda'). Lentils are now a favourite food of mine, and I love to match them with Black Pig belly bacon and the freshest, greenest extra virgin olive oil I have.

SERVES 4

½ cup (100 g) organic puy-style lentils
⅓ cup (80 ml) extra virgin olive oil, plus extra for drizzling
sea salt and freshly ground black pepper
30 g traditionally smoked belly bacon, trimmed of skin and cut into 1 cm pieces
1 onion, roughly chopped
3 cloves garlic, finely chopped
1 tablespoon rosemary leaves, roughly chopped
¼ cup (60 ml) verjuice
2 tomatoes, diced
2 sticks celery, finely diced, pale green leaves roughly chopped and reserved
4 sprigs lemon thyme, leaves picked and chopped
handful flat-leaf parsley leaves, roughly chopped
25 g Parmigiano Reggiano (optional), shaved

Place the lentils in a saucepan, cover with 3 cups (750 ml) water and bring to a simmer over medium heat. Cook for 15–18 minutes or until tender, making sure the water does not boil. Drain the lentils, transfer to a bowl and drizzle over half the oil and season with sea salt to taste. Set aside and keep warm.

Heat a non-stick frying pan over medium–high heat, then add the bacon and cook until crisp. Transfer to a plate lined with paper towel to drain, then set aside.

Meanwhile, return the frying pan to medium–high heat and add the remaining oil. Cook the onion for 5 minutes or until golden brown. Reduce the heat to medium, then stir in the garlic and rosemary and cook for 3 minutes. Increase the heat to high, then add the verjuice and cook, stirring, for about 2 minutes or until the verjuice has almost evaporated. Season with a good pinch of sea salt, remove from the heat and add to the warm lentils, along with the reserved bacon, and stir to combine. Set aside to cool for 10 minutes.

Place the tomato, celery, celery leaves, thyme and parsley into a large bowl, season and toss together. Add the cooled lentil mixture and gently stir to combine. Taste and adjust the seasoning, then add an extra drizzle of olive oil if required. Scatter over the shaved Parmigiano just before serving, if using.

Brains in Burnt-butter, Capers and Verjuice Sauce

These days you have to order brains in advance from your butcher and, sadly, they'll nearly always be frozen. Don't let that deter you, however, as this dish, teamed with a glass of chilled Seppeltsfield Flor-Fino sherry, is one of the great food matches of my life. A big statement, I know, but there is something about the creaminess of the brains combined with the finesse of the sherry that makes me salivate even as I write this. It's always best to poach the brains the day before to allow enough time for them to set properly.

SERVES 2 AS A LIGHT MEAL

- 4 sets brains
- 30 g unsalted butter
- 1 tablespoon extra virgin olive oil
- sea salt and freshly ground black pepper
- 2 tablespoons salted capers, rinsed
- ¼ cup (60 ml) verjuice
- 2 tablespoons chopped flat-leaf parsley leaves

To prepare the brains, place in a bowl and cover with cold water. Transfer to the fridge to soak for 2 hours, then drain well. Wrap each set of brains tightly in foil so they hold their shape. Put the foil parcels in a deep-sided frying pan and cover with cold water. Place over high heat and bring to the boil, then immediately reduce the heat to low–medium and simmer for 12 minutes. Remove the foil parcels with a slotted spoon and transfer to a plate, then store in the refrigerator for at least 1 hour to set (although anywhere up to 12 hours is preferable).

When ready to cook, remove the foil from the brains and pat them dry with paper towel. Cut each brain in half lengthways.

Melt the butter in a large frying pan over medium–high heat and cook for 2–3 minutes or until nut-brown, adding the oil when the butter starts to bubble to prevent it from burning. Lightly season the brains then fry them, cut-side down, for 2 minutes before turning them over to cook for 1 minute on the other side. Add the capers and verjuice and cook, stirring, for about 30–45 seconds or until the liquid reduces by half, then scatter over the parsley. Remove from the heat and serve immediately.

Caramelised Fennel with Capers

Now that we can get baby fennel in the summer and beautiful plump fennel through autumn and winter, I find I use it year-round in so many ways. It has a sweet aniseedy flavour when cooked like this and, when finished off with the capers and verjuice, it takes on a lovely salty/sour dimension that is a great foil for rich meat dishes. Alternatively, it can easily become the star of the plate as a luncheon dish, served on toasted sourdough rubbed with garlic and olive oil as a bruschetta topped with dobs of fresh goat's curd.

SERVES 4 AS AN ACCOMPANIMENT OR A LIGHT LUNCHEON DISH

60 g unsalted butter
1 tablespoon extra virgin olive oil, plus extra for drizzling
1 teaspoon sugar
4 bulbs baby fennel, trimmed, cut in half and sliced lengthways into 5 mm thick slices, fronds reserved and roughly chopped (you want about 2 tablespoons chopped fronds)
sea salt
¼ cup (60 ml) verjuice
1 tablespoon salted baby capers, well rinsed
freshly ground black pepper

Melt the butter in a non-stick frying pan over high heat until nut-brown, then add the oil to stop the butter burning. Reduce the heat to medium–high, then sprinkle in the sugar and toss in the fennel. Season with 1 teaspoon sea salt and cook for 6 minutes, stirring every couple of minutes, until slightly caramelised, then remove the fennel from the pan and drain on paper towel.

Wipe the pan with paper towel and place over high heat. Add the verjuice and cook for 3 minutes, stirring, until reduced by half, then return the caramelised fennel to the pan and cook for 1 minute or until most of the verjuice has been absorbed.

Remove the pan from the heat and stir through the capers, fennel fronds and some freshly ground black pepper. Transfer to a serving platter and add a final flourish of olive oil before serving.

Rabbit Broth

This broth featured as part of an adventurous meal I helped put together for a Diggers and Dealers dinner to be served at the mouth of a goldmine in Coolgardie in Western Australia. My brief was to evoke the early days of gold mining using the produce of the surrounding region and, of course, wild rabbits and truffles just happened to fit this bill. We worked from a camp kitchen to produce the food for 80 guests. It would be a total extravagance to use farmed rabbit for this dish. Anyway, I always feel that using wild rabbit helps rid the countryside of a scourge, and tastes so good at the same time. If you find that you've reduced your broth a little too much (ideally you'll have about 1.25 litres after simmering), you can top up the pan with water. The truffle is optional, of course – the freshly chopped parsley and extra virgin olive oil added at the end will still make the dish shine.

SERVES 6

---

2 × 700 g wild rabbits, each cut into eight pieces
¼ cup (60 ml) extra virgin olive oil, plus extra for drizzling
2 brown onions, roughly chopped
2 carrots, roughly chopped
2 sticks celery, roughly chopped
180 g flat field mushrooms, roughly chopped
3 cloves garlic, crushed
50 g pancetta, thinly sliced
100 ml verjuice
600 ml Golden Chicken Stock (see page 190)
1.2 litres Vegetable Stock (see page 191)
1 bay leaf
6 black peppercorns
4 sprigs thyme
10 stalks flat-leaf parsley, plus extra, leaves picked and chopped, to serve
sea salt and freshly ground black pepper
30 g fresh truffle (optional), shaved

Preheat a fan-forced oven to 220°C (240°C).

Place the rabbit pieces on a baking tray, drizzle with olive oil and rub to coat well. Roast for 20 minutes or until nicely browned.

Meanwhile, place a large stockpot over medium–high heat and add the olive oil. When the oil is hot, add the onion, carrot, celery and mushrooms and cook for 10 minutes. Add the garlic and pancetta and cook, stirring regularly, for 5 minutes or until the vegetables are golden brown. Add the verjuice, stirring to remove any caught bits from the base of the pot, and bring to a simmer. Add the chicken stock, vegetable stock, bay leaf, peppercorns, thyme, parsley and the browned rabbit pieces. Bring to the boil, then reduce the heat to low–medium and simmer for 1½–2 hours or until the meat falls off the bone.

Strain the broth through a fine-meshed sieve into a clean saucepan, reserving the front and back rabbit legs and discarding the saddle and other solids. Season the broth to taste and bring to a simmer over medium heat.

Meanwhile, remove the rabbit leg meat from the bones and pull apart with your fingers. Add to the broth and warm through.

Serve the broth in warmed bowls topped with some chopped flat-leaf parsley, a final drizzle of olive oil and some shaved truffle, if using.

Leeks Poached in Verjuice with Olives

Whilst I've always liked leeks, I only became passionate about them when I started to grow some myself, and found nothing beats pulling them from the ground and cooking them immediately. This can be served as a side dish, or you could add generous dollops of Persian feta, fresh ricotta, goat's curd, gruth or quark and serve it with some crusty bread as a luncheon dish. You could also add these poached leeks to a warm salad of roast winter veg, or cut them into small pieces and use them to make a great sandwich with hardboiled eggs mashed with handmade mayonnaise between toasted sourdough.

SERVES 2 AS AN ACCOMPANIMENT OR A LIGHT LUNCHEON DISH

4–6 small leeks (2–2.5 cm diameter)
½ cup (125 ml) verjuice
20 g unsalted butter
sea salt and freshly ground black pepper
⅓ cup (40 g) pitted black olives
extra virgin olive oil, for drizzling
1 tablespoon oregano leaves
chopped flat-leaf parsley (optional), to serve

Trim the tough outer leaves from the dark green part of the leeks. Place the leeks on a chopping board and make a crossways cut through the first 2 cm of the green ends. Carefully trim the roots, leaving about 2 cm intact. Transfer the leeks to a bowl of cold water and leave to soak for 10 minutes to remove all the grit and dirt, then drain and pat dry with paper towel.

Place the leeks in a large frying pan and cover with the verjuice and 2 cups (500 ml) water. Add the butter, salt and a little pepper, then bring to the boil. Cover the leeks with a round of baking paper cut to fit the pan (this ensures the leeks remain submerged). Reduce the heat to low–medium heat and simmer for 15–20 minutes or until the leeks are soft and cooked all the way through but still hold their shape; insert the point of a sharp knife to test. Carefully remove the leeks with tongs or a slotted spoon and drain the excess liquid. Drain well on paper towel, then transfer to a serving dish.

Toss the olives in a little oil and scatter over the leeks, along with the oregano. Drizzle over an extra flourish of oil and serve warm or at room temperature, scattered with chopped parsley, if desired.

Roast Baby Vegetables with Parmesan Polenta

Vegetables are so important to me – they're just as big a star on the plate as the best piece of beef, chicken or fish. I try to have one meal a week that's totally vegetarian, often accompanied with cheese in some form or another, and this is a perfect example. Not that I don't get the odd grizzle from Colin, who was brought up eating meat at every meal, but from the way this dish is eaten with gusto, I can see it's just words! Beetroot does tend to 'bleed' a little when cooking, making it a less vibrant colour, so I leave some of the beetroot stalk attached to minimise this.

SERVES 4 AS AN ACCOMPANIMENT

salt
1 bunch baby (Dutch) carrots, green tops trimmed, leaving about 2 cm stalk intact
6 pickling onions *or* golden shallots, peeled
1 bunch baby beetroot, leaves trimmed, leaving 2 cm stalk intact
⅓ cup (80 ml) extra virgin olive oil, plus extra for drizzling
sea salt and freshly ground black pepper
small handful lemon thyme leaves
½ cup (125 ml) verjuice

PARMESAN POLENTA
1.25 litres milk
sea salt
350 g instant white polenta
¾ cup (180 ml) verjuice
⅓ cup (80 ml) extra virgin olive oil, plus extra for drizzling
½ cup (40 g) grated Parmigiano Reggiano

Bring a saucepan of salted water to the boil over high heat. Add the carrots and cook for 4 minutes, then remove with a slotted spoon and transfer to a colander to drain. Add the onions to the pan and cook for 10 minutes. Once the carrots are cool, rub off their skins with a clean Chux (J-cloth), cut them in half lengthways and transfer to a bowl.

Remove the onions or shallots with a slotted spoon and transfer to a colander to drain. Add the baby beetroot to the pan and cook for 20 minutes or until softened. Meanwhile, peel the onions and cut in half, if desired, then add to the bowl of carrot. Drizzle with 2 tablespoons of the oil, season with salt and pepper and sprinkle with 1 tablespoon of the thyme leaves, then stir to mix through.

Drain the beetroot and leave to cool slightly. Slip off the skins by hand and cut in half, if desired, then place in a separate bowl. Drizzle with the remaining oil, season with salt and pepper and sprinkle with 1 tablespoon of the thyme, then stir to mix through.

Preheat a fan-forced oven to 200°C (220°C) and line two shallow roasting pans with baking paper.

Spread the onions and carrot in one of the roasting pans, then place the beetroot in the second roasting pan. Roast for 15 minutes or until just cooked through and the carrot and onion are turning golden around the edges (the beetroot may need slightly longer). Pour ¼ cup (60 ml) of the verjuice into each pan and return it to the oven to cook for a further 3–5 minutes until the verjuice caramelises.

Meanwhile, to make the parmesan polenta, place the milk, 2 teaspoons salt and 3 cups (750 ml) water in a large heavy-based saucepan, bring to the boil then reduce the heat to low–medium. Stirring continuously, gradually pour in the polenta until it has all been incorporated and cook for 5 minutes or until the polenta has thickened. Stir in the verjuice and, when it has been absorbed, add the oil and cook for 4 minutes. Stir in the Parmigiano, then season with salt and drizzle with oil, if desired. Keep warm.

Combine the onion, carrot and beetroot and toss through the remaining thyme. Serve immediately on a bed of parmesan polenta, drizzled with extra oil (or use any oil remaining in the roasting pans).

Goat's Cheese and Walnut Salad

Up until her retirement a few years ago, West Australian Gabrielle Kervella, a pioneer of Australian cheesemaking, was making the most wonderful cabecou-style goat's cheese rounds that were just perfect served slightly softened on thickly sliced ciabatta. I always had a stock of them in the fridge, and if they became dry because I'd forgotten to use them, they were never wasted. I'd grate them through just-cooked fresh pasta with olive oil, giving it a wonderful sharpness and intensity. Luckily, Woodside Cheese Wrights in Adelaide make similarly delicious rounds, which are available in good delicatessens.

SERVES 4

½ cup (50 g) walnuts
4 × 1.5 cm thick slices ciabatta
200 g soft goat's cheese, divided into 4 rounds
1 clove garlic, cut in half
extra virgin olive oil, for drizzling
100 g mixed young lettuce leaves
edible flowers (optional), to serve

WALNUT VINAIGRETTE
¼ cup (60 ml) walnut oil
¼ teaspoon Dijon mustard
¼ cup (60 ml) verjuice
sea salt and freshly ground black pepper

Preheat a fan-forced oven to 200°C (220°C).

Place the walnuts on a baking tray and roast for 5 minutes or until golden, checking them frequently to make sure they don't burn. Immediately wrap in a clean tea towel and rub to remove the skins. Shake the walnuts in a sieve to get rid of the skins, then set aside to cool.

Heat a chargrill pan to hot and grill the ciabatta until golden on both sides. (Alternatively, place under a hot grill.) Rub the cut garlic clove over the surface of the ciabatta, then drizzle with olive oil.

Place a round of goat's cheese on each piece of toast, then transfer to a baking tray. Bake for 4–5 minutes or until the cheese begins to soften a little and is warmed through.

To make the walnut vinaigrette, whisk the walnut oil, Dijon mustard and verjuice together until combined, then season to taste with salt and pepper.

Divide the ciabatta among four plates, then pile some lettuce leaves alongside. Scatter with the walnuts, drizzle with the vinaigrette and serve, topped with edible flowers, if using.

Jerusalem Artichoke and Ruby Grapefruit Salad

It's not surprising that many of the flavours that go together are from fruit and vegetables that are in season at the same time. While I love Jerusalem artichokes in any form, they do have a reputation for causing flatulence; however, quickly pan-fried like this, I find they don't seem to have the same effect. It's worth a try, as anyone who has eaten Jerusalem artichokes will attest to their fabulous flavour. They do have a tendency to oxidise when cut, so slip the slices into a bowl of water with lemon juice or verjuice added if you're not going to cook them immediately, then dry them thoroughly before cooking. If you have beautifully fresh walnuts, as I did here, you won't need to rub off their skins. You could even dispense with roasting them if you like, as their fresh flavour will enhance the dish. Add prosciutto or grilled pancetta to this salad to make it a more substantial meal.

SERVES 4

½ cup (50 g) walnuts
40 g unsalted butter
extra virgin olive oil, for cooking
4 Jerusalem artichokes, peeled and thinly sliced
1 tablespoon verjuice
1 large ruby grapefruit, peeled and sliced, slices cut into quarters
50 g gorgonzola dolce, broken into small pieces
1 small bunch rocket
micro herbs (optional), to garnish

VINAIGRETTE
¼ cup (60 ml) verjuice
sea salt and freshly ground black pepper
¼ cup (60 ml) walnut oil

Preheat a fan-forced oven to 200°C (220°C).

Place the walnuts on a baking tray and roast for 5 minutes or until golden, checking them frequently to make sure they don't burn. Immediately wrap in a clean tea towel and rub to remove the skins. Shake the walnuts in a sieve to get rid of the skins, then set aside to cool.

Melt the butter in a frying pan over high heat and cook for 2–3 minutes until nut-brown, adding a splash of oil when the butter starts to bubble to prevent it from burning. Add the Jerusalem artichoke, reduce the heat to medium and saute for 5 minutes or until just cooked through and lightly golden. Increase the heat to high, add the verjuice and cook, stirring, for 45 seconds or until the verjuice has evaporated and the artichokes are glazed, then transfer to a bowl.

To make the vinaigrette, place the verjuice in a bowl and season with salt and pepper. Slowly mix in the walnut oil, whisking to combine. Taste and adjust the seasoning.

Add the walnuts, grapefruit, gorgonzola, rocket and some of the vinaigrette to the bowl with the Jerusalem artichoke, and toss to combine thoroughly.

To serve, divide the salad among four plates. Drizzle the remaining vinaigrette over, and scatter with micro herbs, if using.

Steamed Cauliflower with Blue Cheese and Verjuice Sauce

I think cauliflower is such an underrated vegetable. I used to be embarrassed that my favourite way of cooking it was in the microwave, until I read food writer Harold McGee's theory that vegetables cooked this way retain far more nutrients and flavour than those cooked by other methods. Whilst cauliflower and cheese sauce is an age-old combo, the blue cheese in this sauce has such a great bite to it that I prefer it to a plain bechamel any day. The sauce is beautifully thick, so my tip is to be at the table, everyone with knife and fork at the ready, and spoon the sauce over the hot cauliflower at the very last minute. The less it melts, the more I like it!

SERVES 4 AS AN ACCOMPANIMENT

---

1 small head cauliflower (about 400 g), cut into florets
2½ tablespoons extra virgin olive oil, plus extra for drizzling
2 tablespoons finely chopped chervil
2 tablespoons verjuice
½ teaspoon sugar
½ cup (125 ml) thickened cream
60 g blue cheese
2 tablespoons finely chopped flat-leaf parsley
sea salt

Place the cauliflower florets in a medium–large microwave-safe container with ¼ cup (60 ml) water. Cover and cook in the microwave on the highest setting for 6 minutes or until just tender when pierced with a knife. Drain well, then transfer to a bowl and drizzle with 1½ tablespoons of the oil. Set aside.

Place the chervil, the remaining oil, verjuice, sugar and cream in a blender and blend to form a sauce. Crumble the blue cheese over and blend again just until the mixture is smooth.

Place the cauliflower in a bowl, then spoon over the sauce. Scatter over some parsley, add a final drizzle of olive oil, then season with salt and serve at once.

Blue Swimmer Crab Custard

Blue swimmer crabs are part of the Beer family culture. Our shack at Port Parham is sacred ground for catching crabs and sitting around the campfire at night in the winter. To us, nothing seems to come close to the flavour of the blue swimmers that we catch, cook, cool on an old wire mattress frame in the yard and then eat very simply with nothing much more than a drizzle of our extra virgin olive oil, some salt, lemon and crusty bread – and not forgetting a good glass of semillon. But when we've eaten our fill, we carefully handpick the meat from the leftover crabs (reserving the shells to make stock so we don't waste a thing) and then, fuelled by a love of my visits to Japan, I make my own version of *chawanmushi*, a silky, Japanese-style savoury custard that is steamed and eaten as an entree. You'll need the meat from 2–3 blue swimmer crabs for this recipe.

SERVES 8 AS AN ENTREE

---

20 g dried shiitake mushrooms (about 5 mushrooms)
75 ml verjuice
50 g enoki mushrooms
2 teaspoons soy sauce
25 ml mirin
1 teaspoon bonito flakes
20 g unsalted butter
sea salt
1 tablespoon verjuice
4 eggs
2 egg yolks
⅔ cup (150 g) freshly picked crab meat, shredded
handful chervil sprigs
pickled ginger, to garnish

Soak the shiitake mushrooms in the verjuice for 10 minutes to reconstitute, then slice.

Trim the base off the enoki mushrooms (reserving the stems and caps for later), then rinse and place in a large stockpot. Add the shiitake mushrooms, soy sauce, mirin and 3 cups (750 ml) water. Bring to a boil and simmer for 20 minutes or until the liquid has reduced to 400 ml. Remove from the heat, stir through the bonito flakes and set aside to cool before transferring to a jug.

In a large frying pan, melt the butter until nut-brown then add the stems and caps of the enoki mushrooms and ¼ teaspoon salt and cook over medium heat for 1 minute or until lightly golden. Increase the heat to high, add the verjuice and cook, stirring, until the verjuice has evaporated. Place on a paper-towel-lined plate to drain, then combine with the crab meat, season lightly with salt and divide between eight 100 ml ramekins.

Strain the reserved stock through a fine-meshed sieve into a jug, pressing down on the solids with the back of a spoon to extract as much liquid as possible. Beat the egg yolks into the cooled stock to form a custard, then pour through a fine-meshed sieve into the ramekins. Top with chervil sprigs and pickled ginger, then cover tightly with foil.

Place a large bamboo steamer over a wok half-filled with water (or use a steamer that fits snugly over a large saucepan) and bring to the boil over high heat. Reduce the heat to low–medium, place the prepared ramekins into the steamer and cover. Steam for 15 minutes or until just cooked, then serve immediately.

Pan-fried Eggplant with Verjuice, Preserved Lemon and Ginger

Eggplant has to be one of my favourite vegetables, and I never tire of finding new ways to cook it. In summer and autumn I eat eggplant at least two or three times a week. Whilst I'd rather have eggplant from my own garden, this last season was a very difficult summer and, having planted four eggplants of different varieties, only one bore, and shyly at that. When buying eggplant, choose carefully. Look for specimens with very shiny, blemish-free skin that aren't too large. A large eggplant often means lots of seeds and, with this, the possibility of bitterness. Here, it's important to cook the eggplant in batches so as not to crowd the pan, or it will stew instead of fry.

SERVES 6 AS AN ACCOMPANIMENT

---

3 quarters preserved lemon, flesh removed, rind rinsed and thinly sliced
1 cup (250 ml) verjuice
3 eggplants (aubergine), cut into 2–3 cm pieces
⅓ cup (80 ml) extra virgin olive oil
sea salt and freshly ground black pepper
1 × 2 cm piece fresh ginger, peeled and thinly sliced
thyme leaves, to serve

Place the preserved lemon rind and 2 tablespoons of the verjuice in a small bowl. Set aside to soak while you cook the eggplant.

Toss the eggplant with the olive oil to coat well, then season with salt and pepper.

Heat a large frying pan over medium heat. Add one-third of the eggplant and saute, stirring occasionally, until the eggplant is caramel in colour and soft to the touch. Increase the heat to high, add one-third of the verjuice and cook, stirring, until the verjuice has evaporated, then transfer the eggplant to a bowl. Return the pan to the heat and repeat this process with another one-third of the eggplant and one-third of the verjuice.

Strain the preserved lemon, discarding the soaking liquid, and add it to the pan, along with the last batch of eggplant and the ginger. Stir to combine, then cook for 8–10 minutes or until the eggplant is caramelised. Increase the heat to high, then add the remaining verjuice and cook, stirring, until the verjuice has evaporated.

Check and adjust the seasoning, then remove the pan from the heat. Leave the eggplant to cool for 5 minutes, then toss through the thyme leaves and serve.

Baked Red Onion and Fennel with Goat's Curd

I guess I could almost be a vegetarian (if I didn't like meat so much!). I love vegetables in so many different ways that I often eat vegetarian without really thinking about it (although I have to sweet-talk Colin into believing a dish without meat, poultry or fish actually constitutes a 'meal'). If you have this issue in your household, try serving vegetarian meals for lunch – this one fits the bill beautifully. The sweetness of the onion, the slight aniseed flavour of the fennel and the creaminess of the goat's curd create a beautiful balance.

SERVES 4 AS A LUNCHEON DISH

1 large bulb fennel, trimmed and quartered, fronds reserved
⅓ cup (80 ml) extra virgin olive oil, plus extra for drizzling
1 meyer lemon, cut into 6 wedges (optional)
sea salt and freshly ground black pepper
2 red onions, halved lengthways
2 tablespoons vino cotto
¼ cup (60 ml) verjuice
4 thick slices ciabatta
1 clove garlic, halved
150 g soft goat's curd

Preheat a fan-forced oven to 200°C (220°C).

Toss the fennel with 2 tablespoons of the oil in a roasting pan, then add the lemon, if using, and season with salt and pepper. Place the onion halves cut-side down on a baking tray and drizzle with the vino cotto and the remaining oil.

Roast the onion for 35 minutes or until tender, cooked through and the cut-side is burnished. Add the fennel to the baking tray and roast for 20 minutes or until cooked through and golden, then add the verjuice and roast for another 5 minutes.

Meanwhile, grill both sides of the bread on a hot chargrill pan, then rub all over with the cut garlic. Drizzle with a little oil, sprinkle with salt and cut into strips.

Just before serving, place the onion and fennel in a bowl, drizzle over a little olive oil, then season to taste with salt and pepper and toss in the fennel fronds. Divide among four bowls and accompany with a generous dollop of goat's curd. Serve the toasted ciabatta strips alongside.

Zucchini Agrodolce

Who doesn't need recipes for zucchini, particularly if you are a gardener? No other vegetable produces so prolifically, though I now grow the lighter-coloured Italian ridged variety, not only for its superior flavour but also because it's not as abundant, so I only have to pick the small, sweet ones every second or third day. I like to par-boil them, before slicing them lengthways, drizzling with extra virgin olive oil and eating as is or in a salad. This recipe calls for a more mature zucchini (but not more than 13 cm long as they become bitter), and the trick lies in the salting. I can't believe the difference that salting makes to the intensity of flavour. You must almost squeeze it dry after rinsing though, to draw out as much moisture as possible. This dish is especially wonderful served with grilled chicken, fish or lamb.

SERVES 4 AS AN ACCOMPANIMENT

2 tablespoons dried currants
¼ cup (60 ml) verjuice
450 g zucchini (courgettes), cut into 3 cm thick rounds
sea salt and freshly ground black pepper
2 tablespoons pine nuts
¼ cup (60 ml) extra virgin olive oil
1 onion, finely chopped
2 cloves garlic, finely chopped
2 tablespoons roughly chopped mint leaves

Place the currants and verjuice in a small bowl and leave to soak for 1 hour. Spread the zucchini rounds on a wire rack, sprinkle lightly with sea salt and leave for 1 hour, then rinse the zucchini and dry really well with paper towel, pressing down lightly to draw out any remaining moisture.

Preheat a fan-forced oven to 180°C (200°C). Place the pine nuts on a baking tray and roast for 6–7 minutes or until golden, checking them frequently to make sure they don't burn. Set aside.

Heat the oil in a heavy-based frying pan with a tight-fitting lid over medium–high heat. Add the onion and saute for 5 minutes, then add the garlic and cook until golden brown. Add the zucchini and cover the pan with the lid. Reduce the heat to low and cook for 15 minutes, turning the zucchini halfway through the cooking time. Remove the lid and increase the heat to medium–high. Add the currants and any verjuice not absorbed and cook for 1 minute or until the liquid has reduced by half and the zucchini is tender.

Transfer to a serving platter and sprinkle over the pine nuts. Check for seasoning and scatter over the chopped mint at the very last moment.

Creamy Fish Soup

I don't often make a creamy soup these days but there's something wonderful about the flavour of fish stock, fennel and Pernod finished off with cream. Mind you, it must be a good-quality fish stock, and for me that's one made with snapper heads (see recipe on page 191).

SERVES 4

---

80 g unsalted butter
¼ cup (60 ml) extra virgin oil olive, plus extra for drizzling
1 large bulb fennel, trimmed and cut into 5 mm thick slices
2 large waxy potatoes (such as Dutch creams), peeled and cut into 3 cm pieces
sea salt
¼ cup (60 ml) verjuice
¼ cup (60 ml) Pernod
3½ cups (875 ml) Fish Stock (see page 191)
120 g salmon fillet, skin removed and pin-boned
4 raw prawns, peeled and deveined
4 scallops, trimmed and cleaned
¾ cup (180 ml) thickened cream
freshly ground white pepper
chervil leaves (optional), to serve
2 lemons, cut in half and briefly grilled

Melt 40 g of the butter with 2 tablespoons of the oil in a large heavy-based saucepan over medium heat. Add the fennel and cook for 4 minutes, stirring occasionally so that the fennel doesn't brown. Add the potato and cook for a further 2 minutes, then add two good pinches of salt. Add the verjuice and Pernod, increase the heat to high and cook for 3–4 minutes, stirring, until the liquid has reduced by about half.

Pour in the fish stock and bring to the boil, then reduce the heat to low–medium and simmer for 30–40 minutes or until the fennel and potato are very tender. Stir through the cream, then, using a stick blender, puree the soup until smooth (if you'd like an even silkier texture, press it through a fine-meshed sieve afterwards). Taste and adjust the seasoning with salt and white pepper if needed, then cover and keep warm.

Heat the remaining butter and oil in a non-stick frying pan over medium–high heat until the butter has melted. Reduce the heat to medium, then add the salmon and cook for 2–3 minutes on each side (depending on the thickness) or until it is cooked one-third of the way through and is still pink in the centre. Transfer the salmon to a paper-towel-lined plate to drain. Add the prawns and scallops to the pan and cook for 1½–2 minutes on each side or until just cooked through, then transfer to the plate with the salmon. Gently flake the salmon into chunks.

Ladle the soup into bowls, then divide the salmon and seafood among the bowls and garnish with chervil, if using. Finish with a final drizzle of oil, then serve with grilled lemon halves alongside.

Pumpkin and Leek Frittata with Gruth

A frittata is a handy thing to have in your repertoire. It's the meal you can have when you're running late home and know you have a few vegetables and herbs in the crisper – if not your own garden – and staples such as eggs and cream in the fridge. And if you've had time to pick up some soft cheese such as gruth or goat's curd on the way home, you can turn this into something really special. It's important to have the right-sized pan for a frittata (mine is 20 cm in diameter and 3 cm deep). Choose one that is ovenproof, so you can finish off the cooking in the oven to give the frittata that lovely puffed look. To me, it's as important as having a good omelette pan.

SERVES 4 AS A LUNCHEON DISH

---

1 large kipfler (about 160 g) or other waxy potato, scrubbed
salt
140 g ripe pumpkin, peeled, seeded and cut into 2 cm dice
¼ cup (60 ml) extra virgin olive oil, plus extra for drizzling
sea salt and freshly ground black pepper
2 sprigs thyme, leaves picked
2 tablespoons verjuice
40 g unsalted butter
1 leek, white part only, sliced
4 eggs
1 tablespoon grated Parmigiano Reggiano
small handful flat-leaf parsley leaves, roughly chopped, plus extra to serve
70 g gruth (see page 24), quark, ricotta or goat's curd

Cook the potato in a saucepan of boiling salted water for 20 minutes or until just tender but not cooked through. Drain, peel and cut into 2 cm dice.

Preheat a fan-forced oven to 220°C (240°C).

Place the pumpkin and potato in a large baking dish, drizzle with 2 tablespoons of the olive oil and season with salt and pepper. Sprinkle with thyme and roast in the oven for 12 minutes or until just cooked through. Pour in the verjuice, then roast for another 3 minutes.

Melt 20 g of the butter in a large heavy-based non-stick frying pan, then add 2 teaspoons of the oil and the leek. Cook for 10 minutes, stirring occasionally, until softened. Transfer to a large bowl and set aside.

Lightly whisk the eggs in a bowl, then stir in the Parmigiano. Add the roast potato and pumpkin to the leek, stir in the parsley and then pour over the beaten egg. Season with a little more salt and pepper and stir to combine well.

Melt the remaining butter in a heavy-based frying pan over high heat and tilt to coat the sides in butter. Pour the frittata mixture into the hot pan; it should puff and frill around the edges. Reduce the heat to low and cook for 3 minutes or until the top is still moist and the underside is golden (carefully lift up the edge of the frittata with a spatula to check).

Transfer the frittata to the oven and cook for 2 minutes to set the top.

Dollop the gruth on top and return to the oven for a minute or so to warm the cheese. Sprinkle with extra chopped parsley and drizzle with oil, then serve.

Sonja Edridge's Mustard-beef Sandwich with Cherry and Ginger Jam

Sonja and I met through our shared love of verjuice many years ago. She is a very talented food stylist and caterer working in London, so when I launched *Maggie's Harvest* in the UK, I asked her to prepare the food. She presented a series of small tastings, all prepared using verjuice, and I'm thrilled to include one of these dishes here. You'll need to marinate the meat overnight to allow the flavours to develop. The cherry and ginger jam is a wonderful accompaniment to savoury dishes (I like to use it with duck, see page 103). If you can't get hold of fresh cherries, make this with canned morello cherries instead. This is a pretty runny jam, so if you prefer it slightly more set, add a good squeeze of lemon juice and boil it for a bit longer: it will thicken and darken, and the aroma of the cherries will not be quite as evident. Once opened, it will keep in the fridge for a few weeks (but this kind of jam tends to crystallise if kept in the fridge too long, so eat it up quickly!). At the Farmshop, we don't sterilise jars when we're making very hot (above 82°C) jams or chutneys – the heat from the mixture is sufficient. Just start with jam jars and lids that are super clean, and then seal and invert the jar once the mixture has been poured in.

SERVES 8 AS A LIGHT MEAL

1 × 1.4 kg beef brisket
40 ml extra virgin olive oil
1 loaf sourdough ciabatta, cut into 1.5 cm thick slices
few handfuls rocket or baby spinach leaves, to serve
sliced pickles, to serve

MARINADE

½ cup (125 ml) verjuice
¼ cup (70 g) Dijon mustard
1 × 2 cm piece ginger, peeled and finely grated
1 tablespoon soft brown sugar
2 teaspoons fennel seeds
sea salt and freshly ground black pepper

CHERRY AND GINGER JAM

1 kg cherries, pitted over a bowl to catch the juices
200 g sugar
1 × 3 cm piece ginger, finely grated
1 cup (250 ml) verjuice
lemon juice, as needed
1 sprig rosemary, leaves picked and chopped

First, make the cherry and ginger jam. Put a few saucers in the freezer, ready to use for testing the jam later. Place the cherries in a food processor and briefly pulse to crush slightly. Place the cherries and their juices, sugar and ginger into a large stainless-steel stockpot or preserving pan over medium heat, stirring occasionally until the sugar has dissolved. Add the verjuice and bring to the boil, then boil rapidly for 15–20 minutes.

To test whether the jam has set, place a teaspoonful onto a chilled saucer. Leave to cool for 1 minute and then push an index finger through it; if the jam wrinkles, it is ready. If it is ready, transfer it to sterilised jars, then seal and invert immediately and leave to cool completely before using. If the jam is not ready, boil for another 10 minutes, then test again (adding a little lemon juice can help it to set).

To make the marinade, place all the ingredients in a screw-top jar, secure the lid tightly and shake well to combine.

Place the beef in a shallow dish and pour the marinade over, massaging it into the meat for 1 minute. Cover with plastic film and refrigerate overnight.

The next day, remove the beef from the fridge 2 hours before cooking.

Preheat a fan-forced oven to 130°C (150°C). Remove the beef from the marinade, shaking off any excess and reserving the marinade.

Place a large enamelled cast-iron (or other heavy-based) casserole over high heat, add the olive oil and, once hot, add the beef and seal for 3 minutes on each side, then pour over the reserved marinade. Cover with the lid, then transfer the casserole to the oven to cook for 3 hours or until the beef is pull-apart tender, turning every 45 minutes. (The cooking time will vary with different ovens: the beef could take anywhere from 2½–4½ hours, so make sure you check it often.)

Remove the beef from the oven and allow to cool slightly in its juices, then transfer to a chopping board and gently pull apart using your fingers.

Meanwhile, toast the bread slices. Serve piled high with beef, rocket or spinach leaves, pickles and some cooking juices spooned over, with the cherry and ginger jam to the side.

MIDDLE

Pumpkin Pizza with Olives and Bocconcini

We have a large wood-fired oven, too large to fire up unless we have a lot of people to cook for, and then the number one request is always pizza. Making pizzas is all about the interaction that occurs: I often have all the ingredients laid out for guests to create their own designs (I say designs because I notice that often the decisions are driven by colour rather than flavour, especially with my grandchildren!). If you're cooking in a conventional oven, a pizza stone is a must for a nice crisp crust: these cost around $15 and are available from kitchen shops and outdoor stores. My other tip is to make the dough in advance: divide into equal portions, roll into balls, cover with plastic film and store in the fridge until needed.

MAKES 6–8

---

600 g ripe pumpkin, peeled, seeded and cut into 1.5–2 cm pieces
½ cup (125 ml) extra virgin olive oil
sea salt and freshly ground black pepper
¼ cup (60 ml) verjuice
500 g fresh bocconcini or fior di latte, cut into 2 cm pieces
60 g pitted kalamata olives
flat-leaf parsley leaves, to serve

PIZZA DOUGH
15 g fresh yeast *or* 2 teaspoons dried yeast
½ teaspoon white sugar, if needed
1¼ cups (310 ml) lukewarm water
500 g unbleached strong plain flour, plus extra for dusting
2 tablespoons whole milk powder
¼ cup (60 ml) extra virgin olive oil, plus extra for greasing
polenta, for dusting

First make the pizza dough. If using fresh yeast, combine with the ½ teaspoon sugar and 1 tablespoon of the warm water in a small bowl, dissolving the yeast with your fingers or mashing it with a fork. Set aside for 5–10 minutes or until foamy.

Mix the flour, milk powder and 1½ teaspoons salt in a large bowl, then make a well in the centre and add the olive oil and yeast mixture (or dried yeast). Pour in the remaining warm water and stir until well combined, then turn the dough out onto a lightly floured bench and knead for 10 minutes or until shiny and smooth.

Place the dough in a well-oiled bowl. Cover the bowl with plastic film and leave in a draught-free spot for 1–1½ hours or until doubled in size.

Turn the dough out onto a lightly floured bench, then knock it back and knead again for a few minutes. Divide the dough into 6 or 8 equal portions. (At this point you can cover the dough and store in the fridge, if making in advance.) Roll each piece into a ball and leave to rest under a damp tea towel for 15 minutes. Using a rolling pin, roll out each ball of dough to a thickness of 1 cm.

Meanwhile, preheat a fan-forced oven to 240°C (240°C).

Toss the pumpkin in ¼ cup (60 ml) of the olive oil, then season with the salt and pepper. Spread the pumpkin on a heavy-based baking tray with a lip, making sure not to crowd it. Roast for 20 minutes or until golden brown, then drizzle with verjuice to deglaze. Roast for a further 5 minutes, then set aside to cool.

Working in batches, stretch each piece of dough by resting it over the back of your hands, with clenched fists and your knuckles pressed together. Gently pull your hands apart, allowing the weight of the dough to stretch itself. (This step keeps the air in the dough, making for a lighter pizza crust.) Alternatively, roll the dough a little thinner with a rolling pin. Lightly dust a pizza tile or heavy-based baking tray with polenta and lay the dough on it. Repeat with the remaining dough.

Lightly drizzle the trays of dough with oil and par-bake for 7 minutes or until golden underneath and puffed. Sprinkle over some bocconcini, then top with the pumpkin and olives (the crust will deflate slightly when it is covered with the topping). Bake for another 10–12 minutes or until the cheese is bubbly and golden.

Sprinkle the pizzas with parsley and add a last flourish of oil, then slice and serve at once.

Mussels in Verjuice with Tomato Sugo

Mussels make for such a quick, easy dinner. They're incredibly inexpensive, full of flavour and readily available. I have to admit to particularly loving Kinkawooka's very small 'petit bouchon' mussels from Port Lincoln, which are available from early June through to late September. They may be small, but they are packed with sweet, intense flavour. Buy a good-quality tomato sugo for this dish as, along with a final flourish of your best extra virgin olive oil, it will make all the difference! You'll have dinner on the table in 15 minutes flat.

SERVES 4

⅓ cup (80 ml) verjuice
½ cup (125 ml) Fish Stock (see page 191) or water
1 kg black mussels, cleaned and beards removed
¼ cup (60 ml) extra virgin olive oil, plus extra for drizzling
2 cups (500 ml) tomato sugo
handful roughly chopped flat-leaf parsley
freshly ground black pepper
crusty bread, to serve

Combine the verjuice and fish stock or water in a large deep frying pan. Bring to the boil over high heat, then immediately add the mussels. Cover with a lid and bring back to the boil. Remove the lid and cook for 3–5 minutes, taking out each mussel the moment it opens and transferring it to a serving dish. After 5 minutes, remove any mussels that haven't opened and, taking care not to burn yourself, carefully prise them open with a knife and smell them; if they smell good, they will be. Add to the dish of opened mussels.

Strain the cooking liquid through a fine-meshed sieve or muslin into a clean saucepan, discarding the solids. Add the oil and tomato sugo, then bring to a simmer over medium heat and cook for 5 minutes. Add the mussels to the pan.

Scatter with parsley, season generously with pepper and finish with a final drizzle of oil, then serve with crusty bread.

Beetroot Risotto

It was my friend Stefano de Pieri who said to me years ago, 'Why aren't you using verjuice instead of white wine to deglaze the pan in your risottos?', and ever since, that's exactly what I've done. If you like, you can reserve 1 cup (250 ml) of the beetroot cooking liquid to add to this risotto, but taste it first – if the beetroot is old, the liquid will be too earthy. If you decide to use it, keep it warm on the stove and add it just before you start adding the stock. If you are using bacon, it's worth seeking out traditionally smoked belly bacon from specialty suppliers if you can (I use my daughter Saskia's Black Pig brand, made from Berkshire heritage-breed pigs). You only need a small amount, and it adds a beautiful smokiness to the dish – a lesser bacon will not add this dimension!

SERVES 6

---

3 large (500 g) beetroot, leaves trimmed leaving at least 1 cm stalks attached
1 litre Golden Chicken Stock (see page 190)
100 g unsalted butter, chopped
⅓ cup (80 ml) extra virgin olive oil, plus extra for drizzling
1 rasher (20 g) traditionally smoked belly bacon (optional), trimmed of skin and chopped
1 large onion, roughly chopped
2 cloves garlic, finely chopped
2 cups (400 g) risotto rice
½ cup (125 ml) verjuice
sea salt
2 sticks celery, finely sliced
75 g coarsely grated Parmigiano Reggiano
1 tablespoon horseradish cream (optional)
small handful chopped flat-leaf parsley leaves
lemon wedges, to serve

Wash the beetroot thoroughly then place in a saucepan of salted water. Bring to a simmer over high heat, then reduce the heat to medium and cook, covered, until they are just tender when tested with a sharp knife or skewer (depending on the size of the beetroot, this could take anywhere from 40 minutes to an hour or more).

Drain the beetroot, reserving 1 cup (250 ml) of the cooking liquid, if using young beetroot. When cool enough to handle, slip the skins off by hand, then coarsely grate the flesh into a bowl and set aside.

Bring the stock to the boil in a saucepan and keep warm. If using the reserved cooking liquid, keep it warm over low heat.

Meanwhile, melt the butter with 2 tablespoons of the olive oil in a heavy-based saucepan over medium heat, then add the belly bacon, if using, and cook for 1 minute. Add the onion and saute for 5 minutes, then add the garlic and cook for 2 minutes or until lightly golden.

Add the rice and stir to coat, then increase the heat to high. Make a well in the centre of the rice, then add the verjuice and cook, stirring, until the verjuice has evaporated. Stir in 2 teaspoons salt. Reduce the heat to medium and add the reserved cooking liquid, if using, and then the hot stock, a ladleful at a time, stirring continuously and waiting for each addition to be absorbed before adding the next.

When you have used two-thirds of the stock, stir in the grated beetroot and check for seasoning. Add another ladleful of stock, then stir in the celery. Add the remaining stock, then continue to cook until the rice is al dente and the mixture is thick and syrupy: the total cooking time should be about 20 minutes.

Stir in the remaining oil, grated Parmigiano and the horseradish cream, if using. Scatter over the parsley and finish with a drizzle of oil and some freshly ground black pepper. Accompany with lemon wedges to squeeze over.

Moussaka

This is a great dish for feeding a crowd. The recipe can be doubled (or even tripled) and made in advance to serve as part of a buffet for people to help themselves, without any pressure on the cook when it comes time to eat. I love the sense of largesse it gives. By the way, it's actually better to make the moussaka the day before as its flavour improves on standing: just keep it in the fridge, then bring to room temperature before warming it for 30–40 minutes in a preheated 160°C fan-forced (180°C) oven. I like to fossick around in second-hand shops for old enamel basins to cook dishes such as this in. You can serve this direct from the dish, accompanied by a huge bowl of bitter leaves dressed with a good vinaigrette.

SERVES 8

½ cup (125 ml) extra virgin olive oil
1 onion, finely chopped
1 clove garlic, crushed
500 g lean minced lamb
1 tablespoon tomato paste
½ teaspoon ground cinnamon
1 cup (250 ml) red wine
sea salt and freshly ground black pepper
2 tablespoons lemon thyme leaves
600 g ripe pumpkin, peeled, seeded and cut into 2.5 cm chunks
3 eggplants (aubergine, about 900 g), trimmed and cut into 1.5 cm thick slices
¼ cup (60 ml) verjuice
olive oil spray, for greasing
3 tablespoons chopped flat-leaf parsley leaves
1 quantity Bechamel Sauce (see page 192)
¼ cup (20 g) finely grated Parmigiano Reggiano

Heat 2 tablespoons of the oil in a large non-stick frying pan over medium heat. Cook the onion for 5 minutes, then add the garlic and cook for 5 minutes or until softened and lightly golden. Increase the heat to high, then add one-quarter of the meat and cook for 8 minutes or until browned, stirring with a wooden spoon to break up any lumps. Push the meat to one side of the pan and repeat with the rest of the meat, browning a quarter at a time until all the meat has been browned. Stir in the tomato paste and cinnamon until well combined. Pour in the red wine and bring to the boil. Season to taste with salt and pepper, then add the lemon thyme. Reduce the heat to low–medium and simmer for 15 minutes or until the liquid has almost evaporated. Remove from the heat and set aside.

Preheat a fan-forced oven to 240°C (240°C). Arrange three shelves in the oven: top, middle and bottom.

Spread the pumpkin on a baking tray lined with baking paper and drizzle with 2 tablespoons of the oil, then brush the eggplant slices on both sides with the remaining oil. Spread the eggplant out in a single layer on two baking trays lined with baking paper. Place the trays of eggplant on the top two oven shelves and the tray of pumpkin on the lower shelf. Bake the eggplant for 10 minutes or until light brown, then turn and cook for another 10 minutes. Bake the pumpkin for 20 minutes or until it begins to turn golden around the edges and is soft to the touch. Remove the eggplant and pumpkin from the oven and drizzle with the verjuice, then return to the oven for 5 minutes. Set aside to cool for 10 minutes, then place the pumpkin in a food processor and puree until smooth.

Reduce the oven temperature to 200°C fan-forced (220°C). Spray a baking dish (mine is 25 cm × 18 cm × 5 cm deep) with olive oil spray. Line the base with half of the eggplant, then sprinkle over 1 tablespoon of the parsley. Evenly spread the minced lamb mixture over the top and sprinkle with another tablespoon of the parsley, then spread half of the bechamel sauce over the top. Layer the remaining eggplant over the bechamel, then sprinkle with the remaining parsley. Spread the pureed pumpkin over the eggplant, then spread with the remaining bechamel sauce for the final layer. Sprinkle with the Parmigiano, then bake for 20–25 minutes or until golden and heated through.

Leave the moussaka to cool slightly, then cut into pieces and serve.

Double-lamb Cutlets with Quince Glaze and Celeriac Remoulade with Pomegranate

You'll have to ask your butcher to cut these chops for you especially, but it's worth the trouble. The thickness of the meat means they are sweet and juicy, and you also get that double quantity of quince-burnished fat that I find irresistible. If you don't have a hood on your barbecue, you can finish the lamb chops in a preheated 200°C fan-forced (220°C) oven for 10 minutes. I have borrowed from Damien Pignolet's wonderful book *French* for the remoulade, though I have added verjuice and pomegranate seeds because I have both in abundance. The remoulade makes double the amount you need for this recipe but it's great the next day too, maybe served with some smoked duck breast for a light lunch.

SERVES 6

6 double-lamb cutlets (about 165 g each), fat left on
¼ cup (60 ml) extra virgin olive oil
sea salt

QUINCE GLAZE

¼ cup (60 g) quince paste
½ cup (125 ml) verjuice
2 teaspoons soy sauce
2 teaspoons sesame oil

CELERIAC REMOULADE

2 small–medium celeriac (about 500 g), peeled and grated
2 tablespoons verjuice
1 small clove garlic, peeled and smashed with the flat of a knife
2 egg yolks
1 tablespoon Dijon mustard
sea salt and freshly ground white pepper
¾ cup (180 ml) extra virgin olive oil
lemon juice, to taste
⅓ cup pomegranate seeds
2 tablespoons chervil leaves

To make the remoulade, in a large bowl toss the grated celeriac with the verjuice to coat (this prevents the celeriac browning).

Rub the inside of a medium-sized mixing bowl with the garlic, then discard the debris. Add the egg yolks, mustard, ¼ teaspoon salt and a few grindings of pepper, then whisk in the oil a little at a time to make a thick mayonnaise. As the sauce thickens, add a little lemon juice (this will sharpen the taste and loosen the texture) and more oil, if necessary to keep the sauce thick. Season to taste and set aside.

Pour off any excess liquid from the celeriac, pat dry with paper towel and transfer to a clean bowl. Spoon in enough sauce to coat it well (but do not smother it), reserving any leftover sauce for another use. Cover the bowl and leave for a few hours, preferably at room temperature, for the flavours to mature.

To make the glaze, heat the quince paste and verjuice in a small saucepan over medium heat, stirring to melt the quince paste, then bring to the boil. Cook for 2–3 minutes to reduce a little; it should have the consistency of runny honey. Remove the pan from the heat and stir in the soy sauce and sesame oil, then leave to cool to room temperature (the glaze will thicken as it cools).

Preheat a barbecue grill plate to high. With a sharp knife, score the fat on the cutlets, then brush the glaze all over the cutlets, drizzle with the olive oil and sprinkle with salt.

Cook the cutlets, fat-side down, for 5 minutes to colour, then seal for a minute on each side, making sure that each part of the cutlet has been sealed. Close the hood of the barbecue and cook the cutlets for 10 minutes (for medium–rare), or to your liking.

Remove the cutlets and transfer to a plate. Loosely cover with foil and leave to rest for 8 minutes.

Scatter the pomegranate seeds and fresh chervil over the celeriac remoulade and serve, spooned onto plates, alongside the lamb cutlets.

< Spaghetti with Globe Artichokes

For this, you'll need to buy roasted artichokes that have been marinated in extra virgin olive oil (on no account should they have touched vinegar!). It's best to drain and serve pasta immediately, but if you can't, drizzle it with olive oil and spread it out on a plate to cool (do not rinse it). Then, when you're ready to serve, just cover it with plastic film and briefly warm in the microwave.

SERVES 2

- 200 g spaghetti
- extra virgin olive oil, to moisten
- 40 g unsalted butter
- 6 globe artichoke hearts, quartered
- 1–2 tablespoons verjuice
- sea salt and freshly ground black pepper
- 1 tablespoon chopped flat-leaf parsley leaves
- 25 g Parmigiano Reggiano, shaved

Cook the pasta in a large saucepan of boiling salted water following the instructions on the packet, then drain and transfer to a bowl. Drizzle over some oil to moisten.

Meanwhile, melt the butter in a frying pan over medium–high heat and cook for 2–3 minutes or until nut-brown, adding 1 tablespoon oil when the butter starts to bubble to prevent it from burning. Toss in the artichoke and cook for 3–4 minutes or until golden and caramelised around the edges, then add the verjuice and cook, stirring, for 2 minutes or until almost all the liquid has evaporated. Add the hot pasta and remove the pan from the heat, tossing to coat the pasta with the sauce. Drizzle with some more oil, season well, then serve scattered with parsley and shaved Parmigiano.

Last-minute Pasta

This is a dish for those days when you've not had a moment to think about dinner. It all depends on a well-stocked pantry: good-quality dried pasta (I use stoneground wholegrain Pangkarra penne from Clare in South Australia), a tin of tuna (Sirena is a good standby) and, of course olives and extra virgin olive oil. With some freshly picked flat-leaf parsley – oh, and a slab of Parmigiano Reggiano in the fridge always helps – you can have a really tasty dinner on the table in 15 minutes.

SERVES 4

- ¼ cup (60 ml) extra virgin olive oil
- 1 brown onion, roughly chopped
- 1 clove garlic, finely chopped
- ¼ cup (60 ml) verjuice
- 2 × 400 g cans crushed tomato
- 2 teaspoons sugar
- ½ cup (80 g) kalamata olives, pitted
- 2 quarters preserved lemon, flesh removed, rind rinsed and finely chopped
- ½ teaspoon freshly ground white pepper
- sea salt
- 400 g penne or rigatoni
- 1 × 425 g tuna in oil, drained and carefully pulled apart
- roughly chopped flat-leaf parsley and shaved Parmigiano Reggiano, to serve

Heat 1 tablespoon of the oil in a frying pan over medium heat. Add the onion and cook for 8 minutes or until light golden. Add the garlic and cook for 2 minutes. Add the verjuice and cook, stirring, for 1 minute, then add the crushed tomato and sugar and cook for 4 minutes. Add the olives and the preserved lemon and cook for 4 minutes. Season with ½ teaspoon white pepper and salt to taste, then remove the pan from the heat.

Meanwhile, cook the pasta in a large saucepan of boiling salted water following the instructions on the packet, then drain.

Add the tuna and cooked pasta to the pan and gently toss to combine. Drizzle over the remaining olive oil and scatter with the chopped parsley and some shaved Parmigiano, then serve.

Leek and Eggplant Tarte Tatin

I've often made the mistake of planting all my leeks at once, so I tend to pick the thin sweet leeks at the beginning of the season, and the much plumper ones at the end. As long as you catch them before they become woody, this is a great dish for the fattest, yet still freshest, leeks you can find.

SERVES 6

2 small eggplants (aubergines), cut into large chunks
1 quantity Sour-cream Pastry (see page 193)
extra virgin olive oil, for cooking and drizzling
2 leeks, trimmed and washed, white parts cut into slices 3 cm thick
¼ cup (60 ml) verjuice
sea salt and freshly ground black pepper
1 tablespoon chopped lemon thyme
1 tablespoon chopped marjoram
torn mint leaves, to serve
120 g goat's curd, to serve

SUGAR SYRUP
1½ tablespoons sugar
½ cup (125 ml) verjuice
1 tablespoon vino cotto

Place the eggplant in a bowl of salted water and leave to soak for 30 minutes; this reduces the amount of oil the eggplant absorbs when it is fried.

Divide the sour-cream pastry in two, with one piece slightly larger than the other. Wrap both pieces in plastic film. Chill the larger piece in the refrigerator for at least 20 minutes and freeze the other piece for another use.

Preheat a fan-forced oven to 180°C (200°C).

Meanwhile, heat 1 tablespoon olive oil in a non-stick 20 cm ovenproof frying pan over medium heat, then add the leek, cut-side down, and cook for 2 minutes before turning over and cooking the other side for 2 minutes or until nicely caramelised. Transfer the pan to the oven and bake for 20 minutes or until the leek is just tender, then remove from the oven and set aside. Increase the oven temperature to 200°C fan-forced (220°C).

Rinse the eggplant and dry in a clean tea towel, then season with salt.

Heat 3 tablespoons olive oil in a non-stick frying pan over medium–high heat and add the eggplant. Cook for 8 minutes, turning occasionally, until golden on all sides, adding a little more oil if needed. Increase the heat to high, then add the verjuice and cook, stirring, for 45 seconds or until the verjuice has evaporated.

To make the sugar syrup, place the sugar, verjuice and ½ cup (125 ml) water in a saucepan and cook over medium heat until reduced and syrupy – you should have about ¼ cup (60 ml) liquid. Stir through the vino cotto and set aside to cool slightly.

Roll out the pastry on a lightly floured bench to 2–3 mm and cut out a round 2 cm larger than the diameter of the frying pan containing the leeks.

To assemble the tarte tatin, scatter the eggplant around the leek in the frying pan, then drizzle with the warm sugar syrup. Add the chopped herbs and cover with the pastry, tucking the edges in. Bake for 10 minutes, then reduce the oven temperature to 180°C fan-forced (200°C) and bake for 20 minutes. Remove from the oven and, when cool enough to handle, invert onto a platter.

Scatter over torn mint leaves and drizzle with a little more oil, then serve with goat's curd alongside.

Corned Silverside with Sugarloaf Cabbage

I know just about everyone used to make their own corned silverside (or corned beef), though now it's something that's been lost to the convenience of the deli counter for many. But for me, bought corned beef will never replace a meal of hot corned silverside, juicily sliced and served with sugarloaf cabbage and perhaps some boiled waxy potatoes. There's a lot of variation in the quality of the corned meat you can buy, so shop around for the best quality. Everyone will have their favourite condiment to go with corned silverside, whether it's mustard, pickles or a white sauce. Richard Gunner, from Coorong Angus Beef, who supplies me with my silverside, told me with great excitement recently that he made a white sauce with verjuice and parsley to go with his corned silverside, and that it was a perfect match. Give it a try!

SERVES 6

¼ cup (60 ml) olive oil
1 × 1.2 kg corned silverside (choose a piece with a good amount of fat), brought to room temperature
3 onions, roughly chopped
2 cloves garlic, roughly chopped
1½ tablespoons soft brown sugar
½ cup (125 ml) verjuice
3 bay leaves
1 teaspoon black peppercorns
boiling water, to cover
1 quantity Bechamel Sauce (optional, see page 192) with 1 tablespoon Dijon mustard stirred through, to serve

SUGARLOAF CABBAGE
2 teaspoons caraway seeds
1 quarter preserved lemon, flesh removed, rind rinsed and thinly sliced
¼ cup (60 ml) extra virgin olive oil
1 kg sugarloaf or savoy cabbage, outer leaves and core discarded, remaining leaves cut into 2 cm thick slices
sea salt and freshly ground black pepper
¼ cup (60 ml) verjuice
small handful roughly chopped flat-leaf parsley leaves (optional)

Heat 2 tablespoons of the oil over medium heat in a heavy-based casserole just large enough to accommodate the silverside. Add the onion and cook for 10 minutes, stirring occasionally until golden brown. Add the garlic and cook for 1 minute, then add the brown sugar. Pour in the verjuice and bring to a sizzling bubble. Add the bay leaves and peppercorns.

Meanwhile, heat the remaining olive oil in a heavy-based frying pan over medium–high heat. Add the silverside, fat-side down, and cook for 3 minutes or until golden brown.

Transfer the meat to the casserole, fat-side up. Add just enough boiling water to cover the silverside, then bring to the boil over high heat. Reduce the heat to low–medium, cover with the lid and simmer for 1¼ hours (if you have a meat thermometer, the internal temperature should register 70°C). Transfer the silverside to a plate, then cover loosely with foil and leave to rest for 20 minutes.

For the sugarloaf cabbage, toast the caraway seeds in a small frying pan over medium heat for 1½–2 minutes or until aromatic and light golden, then set aside. Soak the preserved lemon rind in a small bowl of cold water for 10 minutes, then drain.

Heat the oil in a large heavy-based frying pan over medium–high heat and gradually add the cabbage. Cook for 5 minutes, stirring until it starts to become tender, then season with salt and pepper. Add the verjuice and increase the heat to high, then simmer for 1 minute or until the verjuice is syrupy. Remove the pan from the heat and scatter with the caraway seeds, preserved lemon and parsley (if using), then transfer to a serving bowl.

Serve slices of the silverside with the sauce, if using, and some sugarloaf cabbage.

Chicken Scaloppini with Brussels Sprouts and Burnt-butter Sauce

Brussels sprouts are another underrated (or is it misunderstood?) vegetable and, to my surprise, I've found that cooking them in the microwave is the best way to retain flavour and nutrients (as with cauliflower, see page 49). Try and buy compact sprouts of a similar size that are a fresh, vibrant green and don't have any old leaves visible. I suggest you buy fairly small chicken breasts and 'bash' them out yourself at home rather than buying them this way – it's rewarding and much more fun!

SERVES 4

¾ cup (105 g) hazelnuts
12 large Brussels sprouts, bases trimmed
salt
4 × 180 g free-range chicken breast fillets from a Barossa or other well-brought-up chook, skin-on
⅓ cup (50 g) plain flour
sea salt and freshly ground black pepper
50 g unsalted butter
2 teaspoons extra virgin olive oil
2 tablespoons verjuice
1½ teaspoons chopped lemon thyme

BURNT-BUTTER SAUCE
60 g unsalted butter, chopped
2 teaspoons extra virgin olive oil
1 tablespoon verjuice

Preheat a fan-forced oven to 180°C (200°C).

Place the hazelnuts on a baking tray and roast for 5–6 minutes or until light golden, checking occasionally to make sure they don't burn. Immediately wrap in a clean tea towel, then rub to peel off the skins. Sift the hazelnuts through a sieve to get rid of the skins, leave them to cool, then cut in half and set aside.

Place the sprouts in a large microwave-safe container with 2 tablespoons water. Cover and cook in the microwave on the highest setting for 6 minutes or until just tender when pierced with a sharp knife. Drain well and set aside for 10 minutes or until just cool enough to handle. Separate the leaves from the sprouts.

Place each chicken fillet between two sheets of plastic film and beat with a meat mallet or rolling pin until 7 mm thick. Dust with flour seasoned with salt and pepper, shaking off any excess.

Melt the butter in a non-stick frying pan over high heat and cook for 3 minutes or until nut-brown, adding a splash of olive oil when the butter starts to bubble to prevent it from burning.

Reduce the heat to low–medium. Lightly season the chicken scaloppini with salt, then cook skin-side down for 2 minutes or until light golden. Turn the scaloppini over and cook for 1 minute. Pour off the excess butter and return the pan to the heat. Add the verjuice, scraping the base of the pan to remove any caught bits, and bring to a sizzling bubble, then remove the pan from the heat immediately. Sprinkle the chicken with lemon thyme and leave in the pan to rest (it will continue to cook during this time).

Meanwhile, to make the burnt-butter sauce, melt the butter in a frying pan over high heat and cook for 4 minutes or until nut-brown, adding the olive oil when the butter starts to bubble to prevent it from burning. Working quickly, add the hazelnuts and toss to coat in the butter mixture. Add the verjuice and the Brussels sprout leaves and cook for 45 seconds–1 minute, to warm through and coat in butter sauce. Serve immediately alongside the chicken.

Chook-in-a-pot

I love a dish where I can put all the ingredients in a pot in the oven and forget about it for a couple of hours. The pot I use for this is a handmade La Chamba clay pot from Colombia, and it just fits one smallish bird snugly. Use a similar-sized heavy-based casserole or, if your casserole is large, cook two birds instead (the snug fit is important). Cooked this way at low temperature over a few hours, the meat creates its own juices and is as tender as can be. After cooking, I simply leave the bird to rest and then serve it on a platter. Accompanied by wilted spinach and waxy potatoes boiled in their skins, then mashed with extra virgin olive oil, this will serve two very hungry people (possibly with some left over for sandwiches the next day).

SERVES 2

---

40 g unsalted butter
1 tablespoon extra virgin olive oil
1 brown onion, finely chopped
2 cloves garlic, sliced
1 × 1 kg free-range chook
sea salt and freshly ground black pepper
4 sprigs lemon thyme
zest of 1 orange, removed in thin strips with a vegetable peeler, leaving the bitter pith
¼ cup (60 ml) verjuice

Preheat a fan-forced oven to 120°C (140°C).

Melt the butter with the oil in a cast-iron casserole or flameproof clay pot over medium heat. Add the onion and cook for 5 minutes, then add the garlic and cook for 5 minutes or until light golden.

Season the chook all over with salt and pepper, then add to the casserole and seal for 2 minutes on each side or until lightly coloured all over. Turn the chook breast-side down. Add the thyme, orange zest and verjuice and cook, stirring, for 1 minute. Cover the casserole with the lid and transfer to the oven to cook for 3½ hours or until the meat is falling off the bone.

Remove from the oven, leave to rest in the casserole for 20 minutes, then serve.

Beef Cheeks Braised in Verjuice

I get a little irritated when I read that beef cheeks are no longer in fashion: nonsense! Slow cooking cuts of meat such as these suits winter so beautifully, and I love to assemble the ingredients in my Le Creuset pot in the morning and come home to a kitchen filled with magic aromas at night. Whilst I don't use the best-quality red wine from the cellar when I'm cooking, life is too short to use rubbish wine. You'll need to marinate the meat overnight for this one to allow the flavours to develop. Depending on your time and inclination, you could skip the last step of reducing the liquid down to a syrup if you like and serve the beef cheeks as they are – in which case you'll need plenty of crusty bread to mop up all the juices. I love to serve this dish with Caramelised Fennel with Capers (see page 38).

SERVES 4

4 × 130 g beef cheeks, trimmed
4 cloves garlic, roughly chopped
2 teaspoons juniper berries, crushed
½ star anise
2 tablespoons rosemary leaves, bruised
3 wide strips orange zest, removed with a vegetable peeler, leaving the bitter pith
2 bay leaves
150 ml extra virgin olive oil
4 golden shallots, roughly chopped
1 carrot, roughly chopped
1 stick celery, roughly chopped
sea salt
½ cup (125 ml) verjuice
½ cup (125 ml) red wine
1 cup (250 ml) veal stock or Golden Chicken Stock (see page 190)
2 tablespoons vino cotto
freshly ground black pepper

Place the beef cheeks, garlic, juniper berries, star anise, rosemary, orange zest, bay leaves and 100 ml of the olive oil in a mixing bowl and massage the herbs and spices into the meat. Cover with plastic film and transfer to the fridge to marinate overnight.

Remove the beef cheeks from the fridge 1–2 hours before cooking, to bring to room temperature.

Preheat a fan-forced oven to 160°C (180°C).

Heat the remaining oil in a cast-iron casserole over medium–high heat. Add the shallot, carrot and celery and cook for 12 minutes or until a dark golden brown. Transfer the vegetables to a bowl and set aside.

Meanwhile, remove the beef cheeks from the marinade, place on a clean plate and season with a good pinch of salt. Strain the liquid from the marinade into the casserole, reserving the solids, and heat through over medium heat.

Add the reserved marinade ingredients, then, working in batches, seal half the beef cheeks for 2 minutes each side, then transfer to a plate while you seal the rest. Return all the beef cheeks to the casserole, then increase the heat to high and add the verjuice and the red wine. Cook, stirring, for 5–8 minutes or until the liquid has reduced by half. Add the stock, vino cotto and reserved vegetables, then season with pepper. Cover and transfer to the oven to cook for 2–2½ hours or until the beef cheeks are meltingly tender but still holding their shape.

Remove the beef cheeks from the casserole, then set aside and keep warm. Strain the cooking liquid into a saucepan (discarding the solids) and simmer until reduced to a syrupy consistency. Season and serve with the beef cheeks.

Kale, Preserved Lemon and Pine Nut Tart

I have fond memories of this tart. I planted kale for the first time in my garden when I found out I was going to be filming with Peter Cundall. I'd heard he drank fresh kale juice every day for its marvellous health-giving properties, and I wanted to surprise him by picking the kale and making it especially for him – which I did, and he loved it. Peter stayed the night at our home in the Barossa and it happened to be a Wednesday, which is when my singing group meets. As luck would have it, it was also the day after Peter's 81st birthday, and so we sang *Happy Birthday* to him. As simple and oft-sung as this song is, when sung in three-part harmonies it is quite beautiful, and I know Peter remembers this fondly as well. If you can't get kale, use the same amount of silver beet (Swiss chard) instead; blanch it for 3–4 minutes, and cut down the currants to ½ cup (80 g), soaking them in ¼ cup (60 ml) verjuice.

SERVES 6

---

1 cup (160 g) dried currants
¾ cup (180 ml) verjuice
1 quantity Sour-cream Pastry (see page 193)
⅓ cup (50 g) pine nuts, plus extra to serve
600 g curly kale, tough stems removed
40 g unsalted butter
¼ cup (60 ml) olive oil
4 golden shallots, sliced
1 clove garlic, finely chopped
1 tablespoon finely chopped preserved lemon rind, rinsed
⅔ cup (200 g) light sour cream
4 large eggs
sea salt and freshly ground black pepper

Soak the currants in ½ cup (125 ml) of the verjuice overnight to soften. Alternatively, place the currants and verjuice in a microwave-safe container and microwave on low for 4 minutes, then set aside for 20 minutes to reconstitute.

Wrap the sour-cream pastry in plastic film and chill in the refrigerator for at least 20 minutes.

Preheat a fan-forced oven to 180°C (200°C). Place the pine nuts on a baking tray and roast for 6–7 minutes or until golden, checking them frequently to make sure they don't burn. Remove and set aside. Increase the oven temperature to 200°C fan-forced (220°C).

Grease a 24 cm tart tin with a removable base. Roll out the pastry on a lightly floured bench until 2–3 mm thick, then use to line the tart tin. Cut off the excess pastry around the edge, leaving 5 mm to allow for shrinkage as it cooks (freeze the offcuts for another use). Refrigerate for 10 minutes.

Prick the pastry base with a fork, then line with foil, fill with pastry weights and blind bake for 15 minutes. Remove the foil and weights and bake for a further 10 minutes or until the pastry looks dry. Remove from the oven and set aside to cool.

Reduce the oven temperature to 180°C fan-forced (200°C).

Meanwhile, blanch the kale in a large saucepan of boiling water for 5–10 minutes or until softened (the cooking time will depend on how coarse the kale is). Drain and set aside until cool enough to handle, then squeeze excess water from the leaves and roughly chop.

Melt the butter with the oil in a large frying pan. Add the shallot and garlic and cook, stirring occasionally, over low–medium heat for 5 minutes or until softened. Increase the heat to high, then add the remaining verjuice and cook, stirring, until the verjuice has evaporated. Transfer this mixture to a food processor, add the chopped kale and any remaining liquid and blend to a puree.

Place the kale puree, currants, pine nuts and preserved lemon in a large bowl and stir until well combined. In a small jug, whisk together the sour cream, eggs, salt and pepper, then stir into the kale mixture.

Carefully pour the filling into the tart shell and bake for 35 minutes or until just set in the centre.

Serve straightaway scattered with a few extra pine nuts.

Meatloaf with Tomato Chutney

In our house, meatloaf is always laced with chutney or fruit sauce from the pantry used with gay abandon. To check the meat mixture for seasoning, the norm is to make a small patty, fry it up and have a taste: however, my daughters and grandchildren all join me in tasting it raw. This makes a perfect family dinner, accompanied by some vegies thrown in the oven to bake at the same time (chunks of white sweet potato and pumpkin and whole onion work especially well). If there is any left over, I seem to remember it makes great sandwiches for school with a little pickled cucumber added.

SERVES 6–8

⅓ cup (80 ml) olive oil
1 large onion, finely chopped
4 cloves garlic, finely chopped
1 tablespoon rosemary, finely chopped
3 quarters preserved lemon, flesh removed, rind rinsed and roughly chopped
⅓ cup (80 ml) verjuice
600 g finely ground minced lamb
600 g finely ground minced pork
⅓ cup (110 g) tomato chutney, plus extra for brushing and serving
handful chopped flat-leaf parsley leaves
2 tablespoons lemon thyme leaves
1 egg, lightly beaten
sea salt and freshly ground black pepper
toasted ciabatta, to serve

Heat the oil in a large frying pan over medium heat. Add the onion and cook for 10 minutes or until softened and light golden, stirring occasionally. Add the garlic and rosemary and cook for a further 4 minutes. Remove from the heat and set aside to cool.

Preheat a fan-forced oven to 140°C (160°C).

Place the preserved lemon and verjuice in a blender and blend until a paste forms. Transfer to a large bowl, then add the minced lamb, minced pork, chutney, parsley, lemon thyme, cooled onion mixture and egg. Sprinkle over some salt (I use 1 tablespoon) and season with pepper. Using your hands, mix all the ingredients together until well combined.

Press the mixture into a 1 kg rectangular loaf pan (mine is 21 cm × 11 cm × 5.5 cm, a heavy-based stainless-steel bread tin is ideal) and smooth the surface to form a slightly mounded shape. Brush the top with extra chutney, then place the pan on a baking tray to catch any juices that may spill over during cooking.

Bake the meatloaf for 1 hour 10 minutes or until browned and cooked through (if you have a meat thermometer, the internal temperature should register 58°C). Set the meatloaf aside to rest for 30 minutes. (If using a meat thermometer, the internal temperature should now register 65°C.)

Slice the meatloaf and serve with extra chutney and some toasted ciabatta alongside.

Coorong Angus Beef Rib with Bearnaise Sauce

I've been spoilt by eating Richard Gunner's Coorong Angus beef over the years. It's not only the breed of cattle that's special: his farming practices and selection of animals are of such excellence that he, and producers like him, are to be applauded. In this recipe, the meat needs to marinate for 24 hours before cooking, so be sure to leave enough time for this. A classic bearnaise sauce has no peer when served with rare beef. Whilst I have taken the lead for this recipe from the wonderful chef Damien Pignolet and his book *French*, I hope he will excuse my substitution of verjuice for vinegar in the reduction. It's simply another way of showing how versatile verjuice is.

SERVES 4

---

1 × oven-prepared 3-pin beef rib section
(I used a 1.93 kg Coorong Angus Beef rib section)
sea salt
verjuice, for drizzling

MARINADE
½ cup (125 ml) vino cotto
½ cup (125 ml) extra virgin olive oil
2 tablespoons Dijon mustard
1 tablespoon soy sauce
¼ cup (60 ml) verjuice, plus extra for drizzling
8 sprigs rosemary, leaves picked

BEARNAISE SAUCE
200 ml verjuice
1 golden shallot, chopped
2 tablespoons chopped French tarragon
2 tablespoons chopped chervil
1 sprig thyme
1 bay leaf, crushed
6 black peppercorns
sea salt
150 g unsalted butter, chopped
4 egg yolks
freshly ground white pepper

To make the marinade, mix the vino cotto, olive oil, mustard, soy sauce, verjuice and rosemary in a small bowl. Place the beef in a baking dish and pour the marinade over, then cover with plastic film and marinate in the refrigerator for 24 hours, turning after 12 hours.

Remove the beef from the fridge 1–2 hours before cooking, to bring to room temperature. Remove the beef from the marinade, then pat dry with paper towel and discard the marinade.

Preheat a barbecue grill plate to high. Season all sides of the beef with salt, then place on the hot grill plate and sear for 2 minutes on each side; this will take about 10 minutes in total as the entire surface should be burnished. Lower the barbecue hood, then reduce the heat to medium and cook for 30 minutes, turning the beef every 5 minutes. Alternatively, cook in a preheated fan-forced 160°C (180°C) oven for 1 hour for medium-rare, or until cooked to your liking. Drizzle over some verjuice and leave the meat to rest for 30 minutes, covered loosely with foil.

To make the bearnaise sauce, place the verjuice, golden shallot, 1 tablespoon each of the tarragon and chervil, plus the thyme, bay leaf and peppercorns in a small saucepan over medium heat and season with a pinch of salt. Bring to the boil and simmer for 6–8 minutes or until reduced to 40 ml, taking care that you don't reduce it beyond this point. Remove from the heat and leave to cool, then strain through a fine-meshed sieve into a small bowl.

Melt the butter in a saucepan over high heat and cook for 3 minutes or until nut-brown. Set aside to cool for 5 minutes.

Place the egg yolks and the strained verjuice reduction in a heatproof bowl. Place the bowl over a saucepan filled with simmering water, making sure the base of the bowl does not touch the water. Gradually dribble the nut-brown butter into the egg mixture, whisking continuously. When the mixture starts to thicken, quickly add the remaining butter, whisking continuously until it has all been incorporated; be careful to leave the burnt butter solids in the saucepan and discard. The sauce should be smooth, thick and emulsified.

Remove the sauce from the heat and stir in the remaining tarragon and chervil. Season to taste with salt and pepper. Cover the surface closely with plastic film to prevent a skin forming, then leave to cool to room temperature before serving alongside the beef.

Pumpkin Risotto

The success of this dish depends on getting hold of the best-quality pumpkin. If you can't find pumpkin with ripe, deep ochre-coloured flesh, then don't bother to make this. In fact, I'd go even further than that: I never bother cooking pumpkin unless I find a mature one of this colour (the best indicator of flavour to the naked eye). For this reason, I would say that buying pre-cut pumpkin is preferable, as you can see what you are getting. Whilst Queensland Blue was the pumpkin of my childhood (and I still think that if you find a perfect one, they're top of the tree), jap pumpkins are more readily available and usually of good quality. And don't forget butternut pumpkin, which is a little more forgiving as it's naturally sweeter.

SERVES 6

- 1 kg ripe pumpkin, peeled, seeded and cut into 2 cm chunks
- ⅓ cup (80 ml) extra virgin olive oil, plus extra for drizzling
- 80 g unsalted butter, chopped
- 1 onion, finely chopped
- 1–1.25 litres Vegetable Stock (see page 191) or Golden Chicken Stock (see page 190)
- 2 cups (400 g) risotto rice
- ½ cup (125 ml) verjuice
- sea salt
- 100 g freshly grated Parmigiano Reggiano
- chopped flat-leaf parsley and shaved Parmigiano Reggiano, to serve

Preheat a fan-forced oven to 210°C (230°C).

Toss the pumpkin chunks with half of the oil in a bowl to coat, then spread on a baking tray lined with baking paper and roast for 20–25 minutes or until cooked and coloured but still firm.

Meanwhile, melt the butter with the remaining oil in a heavy-based saucepan over medium heat, then add the onion and saute for 10 minutes or until lightly golden.

Bring the stock to the boil in a saucepan over high heat and keep warm.

Add the rice to the pan with the onion and stir to coat, then increase the heat to high. Make a well in the centre of the rice, then add the verjuice and cook, stirring, until the verjuice has evaporated, and stir in 1½ teaspoons salt. Reduce the heat to medium and add the hot stock to the rice mixture, a ladleful at a time, stirring continuously and waiting for each addition to be absorbed before adding the next.

When you have used half the stock, add half of the roasted pumpkin, using a spoon to mash the pumpkin into the rice a little. Add the remaining stock and continue to cook until the rice is al dente and the mixture is thick and syrupy: the whole cooking time should be about 20 minutes. Stir through the grated Parmigiano and check for seasoning.

Spoon the risotto into serving dishes and top with the remaining roasted pumpkin and a scattering of chopped parsley. Drizzle with more oil and serve with some shaved Parmigiano alongside.

Spiced Chook Marylands

Chicken marylands (thigh and drumstick joints) or chicken thighs, both with skin on, are a definite favourite of mine if I'm not cooking a whole bird. I should put on the record here that I think it's a travesty to cook chicken without skin. The skin is nature's way of protecting the flesh – it keeps the meat moist during cooking and the fat does not penetrate the meat. If you're concerned about fat, you can discard the skin after cooking. Well, that's me off my soapbox for now! The combination of cinnamon, quince and verjuice gives a sweet/sour flavour that permeates the flesh of the chicken, and the sticky paste results in an impressively crispy skin. Chicken marylands vary in size (the ones I used were around 250 g each), so remember to adjust the cooking times accordingly. It's essential to leave enough time to rest the chicken for 15 minutes after cooking – it will make all the difference.

SERVES 6

75 g quince paste
100 ml verjuice
1 tablespoon ground cinnamon
2 tablespoons soft brown sugar
6 chicken marylands (thigh and drumstick joints) from a Barossa or other well-brought-up chook
500 g green beans, topped and tailed
¼ cup (60 ml) extra virgin olive oil

Place the quince paste and verjuice in a small saucepan over low heat, stirring for 2 minutes or until the quince paste melts. Alternatively, place the quince paste and verjuice in a microwave-safe container and heat in the microwave on high for 1 minute.

Place the quince paste mixture, cinnamon and sugar in a large bowl and mix well to form a paste. Add the chicken to the paste, then toss to coat well. Set aside to marinate for 30 minutes, turning the chicken after 15 minutes.

Preheat a fan-forced oven to 200°C (220°C).

Place the chicken on a wire rack sitting over a roasting pan. Roast the chicken for 15–20 minutes, then check; if the skin seems to be burning, pour ¼ cup (60 ml) water into the roasting pan. Roast the chicken for a further 10–15 minutes or until it is just cooked through; the juices will run clear when a skewer is inserted into the thickest part of the flesh. Transfer the chicken to a plate, cover loosely with foil and leave to rest for 15 minutes before serving.

Meanwhile, cook the green beans in a saucepan of boiling salted water for 3 minutes, then drain.

Divide the green beans among six serving plates and drizzle with half the olive oil. Top with a chicken maryland, drizzle over the remaining oil and any juices from the resting chicken, and serve.

Chicken Breast Supremes with Currants, Pine Nuts, Rosemary and Verjuice

How confusing to find that people all over the country have a slightly different name for this cut of chicken, the breast with the skin left on and the wing bone attached. I tend to keep things simple and refer to it as a chicken breast; in some states it's called a supreme, whilst in Victoria it's known as a kiev. Whatever it's called, this dish is as simple as cooking gets, and so tasty too, with the pine nuts and rosemary deglazed in verjuice giving an absolute 'pow' of flavour. If using four smaller breasts, choose a smaller pan and, working in two batches, pan-fry them skin-side down for 6–10 minutes, then turn and cook for another 3–4 minutes or until almost cooked through. Rest them for 10 minutes before serving.

SERVES 4

¼ cup (40 g) dried currants
¼ cup (60 ml) verjuice
¼ cup (60 ml) extra virgin olive oil, plus extra as needed
2 sprigs rosemary, leaves picked
2 large (about 350 g each) chicken breast supremes from a Barossa or other well-brought-up chook, skin-on *or* 4 × 190 g chicken breasts, skin-on
sea salt and freshly ground black pepper
¼ cup (40 g) pine nuts
20 g unsalted butter
soft polenta or potatoes mashed with extra virgin olive oil, to serve

Soak the currants in verjuice overnight (or for at least several hours). Alternatively, place the currants and verjuice in a microwave-safe container and microwave on low for 2 minutes, then set aside for 20 minutes to reconstitute.

Place the olive oil and rosemary in a large bowl, then add the chicken breasts and season. Cover with plastic film and leave to marinate for at least 1 hour at room temperature (if you are marinating them for longer, it's best to refrigerate them, but make sure you bring them to room temperature before cooking).

Preheat a fan-forced oven to 180°C (200°C). Place the pine nuts on a baking tray and roast for 6–7 minutes or until golden, checking them frequently to make sure they don't burn. Remove and set aside.

Melt the butter in an ovenproof frying pan large enough to hold the chicken breasts in one layer and cook for 2–3 minutes over high heat until nut-brown, adding a splash of oil when the butter starts to bubble to prevent it from burning.

Lightly season the chicken on each side with salt. Place the chicken skin-side down in the pan and cook for 3 minutes or until the skin is golden, then turn and cook for another 2 minutes. Transfer the pan to the oven and cook the chicken for 15 minutes or until the juices run clear when pierced with a skewer at the thickest part of the bone.

Transfer the chicken to a plate, skin-side down, and cover loosely with foil. Leave to rest for 10 minutes.

Meanwhile, discard any butter left in the pan and return the pan to medium heat. Toss in the currant mixture and stir to deglaze the pan, scraping up any caught bits. Simmer for a few minutes until the liquid has reduced to a syrup. Stir in the pine nuts to coat with the syrup glaze.

If using large chicken breasts, cut them in half before serving. Divide the chicken among four plates then spoon the glazed pine nuts and currants over. Serve with soft polenta or potatoes mashed with olive oil.

Penne with Burrata and Tomato

I first tasted burrata in Los Angeles in 2007 at Nancy Silverton's then just-opened restaurant, Pizzeria Mozza. I thought I'd died and gone to heaven. Burrata is a fresh Italian mozzarella made from cow's milk that is shaped a bit like a pouch: a firm casing of cheese, tied at the top, surrounding a creamy centre. To me, it was one of the best tastes ever – and there it was, served on a pizza, with very ripe tomatoes roasted in a little vino cotto. Burrata is now made here, both in Victoria and Queensland, and you can also buy an imported product from Italy. Believe me, the search for burrata is worth it for its lusciousness, but if you have no luck, you could use large balls of fresh bocconcini.

SERVES 4

- 400 g penne
- ½ cup (125 ml) extra virgin olive oil, plus extra for drizzling
- 750 g ripe tomatoes, diced
- ⅓ cup (80 ml) verjuice
- sea salt and freshly ground black pepper
- 8 basil leaves (preferably lemon basil)
- 140 g burrata or bocconcini

Cook the penne in a large saucepan of boiling salted water following the instructions on the packet, then drain and drizzle with 2 tablespoons of the olive oil.

Meanwhile, heat the remaining oil in a large frying pan over medium–high heat. Add the tomato and saute for 8 minutes or until it has softened and started to break down. Increase the heat to high, pour in the verjuice and cook, stirring, for 1 minute or until the liquid has reduced slightly. Season with salt and pepper, then stir through the freshly torn basil leaves.

Serve the pasta in warmed serving bowls with the tomato sauce spooned over. Tear some burrata into each bowl and let it spread over the sauce, then finish with a drizzle of olive oil and a grind of pepper and eat immediately.

Turkey Breast with Cumquat Butter

Here I used a free-range corn-fed turkey breast with the wing attached and, can I tell you, they are well worth seeking out. They will cook in less time than a mass-produced turkey breast, so remember to keep this in mind. The cumquat butter not only adds flavour, but also moistness, to the meat. I tend to be particularly extravagant with butter: if you want to cut down the amount in the stuffing, please do so. I use candied cumquats from the Tolley's Kumquatery at Renmark; you could also use fresh cumquats, chopped and squeezed of their juices, or dehydrated cumquats. They all provide a wonderful bittersweet sharpness that goes well with rich meats.

SERVES 4

---

1 × 680 g turkey breast with wing attached (from a well-brought-up, corn-fed bird), skin-on
60 g unsalted butter, chopped
1 tablespoon extra virgin olive oil
2 tablespoons verjuice
mixed leaf salad, to serve

CUMQUAT BUTTER

100 g candied cumquats
100 ml verjuice
150 g unsalted butter, chopped and slightly softened
small handful flat-leaf parsley leaves, roughly chopped
4 sprigs thyme, leaves stripped and chopped
sea salt and freshly ground black pepper

To make the cumquat butter, place the cumquats and verjuice in a small stainless-steel saucepan, then bring to the boil over medium–high heat and simmer for 5 minutes or until the verjuice has reduced to 1 tablespoon of syrup. Remove from the heat and set aside to cool.

Remove the cooled cumquats from the pan, then roughly chop and place in a mixing bowl. Add the verjuice syrup, butter, parsley and thyme. Season to taste with salt and pepper, then stir to mix well and set aside.

Place the turkey breast skin-side down on a chopping board, then cut crossways through the centre, taking care not to cut all the way through, to butterfly the breast and open it out like a book, with the cut-side facing up. Place a sheet of plastic film on top of the turkey and pound it with a meat mallet or rolling pin until 1.5 cm thick.

Spread the cumquat butter evenly over three-quarters of the butterflied turkey breast, leaving a 3 cm border along the skin-side. Roll the turkey up tightly to enclose the butter and form a compact roll, then truss with cooking twine, making sure the skin-side faces up. Tightly wrap the rolled turkey in plastic film, then refrigerate for at least 1 hour (overnight is best); this helps the roll to retain its shape during cooking.

Preheat a fan-forced oven to 160°C (180°C).

Remove the plastic film from the turkey. Melt the butter in a non-stick ovenproof frying pan over medium heat and cook for 3 minutes until nut-brown, adding the olive oil when the butter starts to bubble to prevent it from burning. Add the rolled turkey breast, skin-side down first, then cook, turning often, for 10 minutes or until browned all over.

Transfer the pan to the oven and roast the turkey for 30 minutes or until just cooked through, turning it after 15 minutes; the juices should run clear when pierced with a skewer at the thickest part of the flesh. (If you have a meat thermometer, the turkey is ready when the internal temperature registers 63°C – it will continue to cook when it is resting.) Drizzle the verjuice over the turkey, cover the pan loosely with foil, then rest for 30 minutes. (If using a meat thermometer, test again after 10 minutes; the internal temperature should register 66–67°C.)

Remove the cooking twine, then slice the turkey and serve with the resting juices, if desired, and a mixed leaf salad alongside.

AUX 2 LIONS
ACIERFORGÉ

Duck Breasts with Cherry and Ginger Jam and Braised Witlof

Duck breasts could almost be considered fast food. If bought in a cryovac bag, they can be kept for ages in the fridge, ready for when you need to cook a special meal very quickly. There is no doubt that they just call out for a glaze on the skin, and here I've used Sonja Edridge's Cherry and Ginger Jam (see page 63). The bitterness of the braised witlof makes it a very grown-up vegetable accompaniment that is a great counterpoint to rich meats such as duck.

SERVES 4

---

4 × 170–180 g duck breast fillets, skin-on
boiling water, for pouring
50 g Sonja Edridge's Cherry and Ginger Jam (see page 63)
¼ cup (60 ml) verjuice
½ cup (125 ml) extra virgin olive oil, plus extra for cooking
small handful coriander leaves
1 teaspoon finely chopped ginger

BRAISED WITLOF

4 heads white witlof
50 g unsalted butter
2 teaspoons caster sugar
¼ cup (60 ml) verjuice

Place the duck breasts on a baking tray and slowly pour boiling water over the skin; you will see the pores open and some of the fat will be released (this helps to achieve a crispy skin). Pat dry with paper towel.

Place the jam, verjuice and half of the olive oil in a small bowl, then whisk to combine. Stir in the coriander and ginger. Rub the jam mixture into the skin and flesh of the duck and leave for 20 minutes.

Meanwhile, to make the braised witlof, bring a saucepan of water to the boil over high heat. Add the witlof and cook for 10 minutes, then remove and drain well. Cut the witlof in half lengthways, place cut-side down on paper towel to absorb any excess moisture, then pat dry. Place a non-stick frying pan over high heat, add the butter and melt until it foams, then add the sugar and witlof, cut-side down. Pan-fry for 2 minutes or until burnished. Deglaze the pan with verjuice and continue to cook for 1–2 minutes or until the verjuice has reduced to a syrupy glaze. Set aside and keep warm.

Preheat a fan-forced oven to 200°C (220°C).

Heat a splash of extra oil over medium heat in an ovenproof frying pan large enough to accommodate the duck breasts. Remove the breasts from the marinade and cook, skin-side down, for 3 minutes, then turn and cook for a further 2 minutes. Turn the breasts back over so they are skin-side down, transfer the pan to the oven and cook for 6 minutes. Remove the pan from the oven, cover loosely with foil, then leave the duck to rest in the residual heat of the pan for 10 minutes.

Divide the braised witlof among serving plates, place a duck breast alongside, spoon over a little of the resting juices and serve.

Sicilian-style Broccolini Pasta

Whilst a more organised person might plan every meal to the minutest detail, in truth I'm sometimes so engrossed in my work that I'm surprised when it's time for dinner and all too often I'm caught on the hop. What I do have up my sleeve is a well-stocked pantry, always filled with top-quality dried pasta, and my own vegie garden to pillage, so it takes only minutes to throw a great pasta dish together. (That is, as long as the pantry also has basics like pine nuts, currants and verjuice, of course.) It's all about classic flavours, quickly cooked and totally delicious.

SERVES 2 AS A MAIN OR 4 AS AN ENTREE

¾ cup (120 g) dried currants
⅓ cup (80 ml) verjuice
½ cup (40 g) flaked almonds
2 bunches broccolini, trimmed
sea salt
250 g penne
1 tablespoon extra virgin olive oil, plus extra for drizzling
150 g gruth (see page 24) or fresh firm ricotta
small handful flat-leaf parsley leaves, roughly chopped
shaved Parmigiano Reggiano, to serve
freshly ground black pepper

Soak the currants in verjuice overnight (or for at least several hours). Alternatively, place the currants and verjuice in a microwave-safe container and microwave on low for 2 minutes, then set aside for 20 minutes to reconstitute.

Preheat a fan-forced oven to 200°C (220°C).

Place the almonds on a baking tray and roast for 5–8 minutes or until golden, checking them frequently to make sure they don't burn. Remove and set aside to cool.

Blanch the broccolini in a large saucepan of lightly salted simmering water for 1 minute or until just bright green. Remove with a slotted spoon, reserving the water in the pan, then refresh under cold running water and set aside. Cut the stalks in half.

Return the reserved broccolini water to the boil over high heat. Cook the pasta until al dente following the manufacturer's instructions. Working quickly, drain the pasta and return it to the warm pan.

Meanwhile, place the almonds, the currants and their soaking liquid, and the olive oil in a large frying pan over medium–high heat. Toss to combine and cook for 2 minutes or until hot, then add the broccolini and toss to combine well. Transfer the broccolini mixture to the pasta, then return to the heat for 1 minute to warm through. Remove from the heat and spoon the gruth or ricotta over the pasta, then sprinkle with the parsley and gently toss to combine.

Divide the pasta among warm bowls, then top with shaved Parmigiano. Drizzle with oil, add a good grinding of freshly ground black pepper and serve.

Roast Pheasant with Thyme and Juniper Berries

Whilst I only use the smallest amount of verjuice in this dish, I felt I had to include a recipe here for pheasant. It is, as many of you would know, the reason my whole food career began, and so I suspect I've cooked more pheasant than most. My two big tips for getting pheasant right are: don't overcook it (the cooking time will vary according to the size and sex of the bird – hen birds have plumper breasts), and give it a long resting period after cooking. The meat will be sweet and delicious if cooked with care, and spoilt if not. I like to drizzle the cooked bird with verjuice the moment it comes out of the oven; this is a trick that can be used for all types of poultry. I love to serve this dish in autumn with parsnip mash, chopped ripe pears and braised cavolo nero.

SERVES 2

---

1 × 700 g pheasant
¼ cup (60 ml) extra virgin olive oil
4 sprigs thyme
1 tablespoon juniper berries, bruised
4 bay leaves
zest of 1 orange, removed in thin strips with a vegetable peeler, leaving the bitter pith
sea salt
60 g unsalted butter
1 tablespoon extra virgin olive oil
½ cup (125 ml) verjuice

To prepare the pheasant, cut the tips off the wings with a sharp knife and take the flesh off the wing joint, scraping back to reveal bare bone. Cut through the skin around the thigh and twist the drumsticks to free them a little, but don't remove them completely. Cut crossways through the backbone to remove the legs from the body (the rib cage with breast meat and wings attached).

Combine the olive oil, thyme, juniper berries, bay leaves and orange zest in a small bowl and mix well.

Place the pheasant in a baking dish and pour the marinade over. Massage in well and leave to marinate at room temperature (or in the fridge if it is a particularly hot day) for 20 minutes–3 hours.

Preheat a fan-forced oven to 220°C (240°C). Season the pheasant with 1 teaspoon salt.

Heat a large, heavy-based non-stick frying pan over medium heat, add the butter and olive oil, then cook the pheasant, skin-side down, for 5 minutes or until the skin is a light golden colour. Turn over and cook on the other side for 5 minutes or until light golden.

Transfer the pheasant, skin-side up, to a roasting pan or shallow baking dish and place in the oven. Roast for 5 minutes, then turn both pieces over and return to the oven for a further 5–6 minutes. Remove the legs from the oven, transfer to a warm plate and splash over 2 tablespoons of the verjuice. Cover loosely with foil and set aside to rest. Cook the breast for a further 8 minutes, then check by piercing with a skewer at the thickest part: if the juices run clear, the breast is cooked. If not, return to the oven for 2–3 minutes and test again.

Remove the pan from the oven and pour the remaining verjuice over the breast, cover loosely with foil and set aside to rest for 20 minutes.

Carve the leg and breast meat from the bone and serve with plenty of the resting juices spooned over.

Glazed Leg of Ham

It's important to know that all legs of ham are not created equal, so look for a traditionally smoked one with a good layer of fat – it will make all the difference! You have to be bold here and bake the glaze on the ham until it's truly burnished. I say that because every oven is so different; your ham might need a shorter or longer cooking time than mine. You'll find your family and friends fighting over the slices that are rimmed with the glazed fat. If you're cooking this for Christmas and have a turkey too, you can place the skin of the ham over the breast of the turkey to keep the meat moist during cooking. Any leftover glaze can be kept in the refrigerator in a sealed container and brushed over a leg or saddle of lamb prior to cooking.

SERVES 16

---

100 g quince paste, chopped
1 cup (250 ml) verjuice
1 × 6 kg leg of ham, traditionally smoked

Preheat a fan-forced oven to 240°C (240°C).

Place the quince paste and verjuice in a small saucepan over high heat and stir to melt the paste. Bring to the boil and cook for 5 minutes or until syrupy. Remove from the heat and set the glaze aside to cool.

Cut away the leathery skin from the top of the ham, taking care not to remove too much fat with it; you are after a 5 mm–1 cm layer of fat left on the ham. Score the fat quite deeply into a diamond pattern, taking care not to cut through to the meat.

Brush several layers of the glaze over the top and sides of the ham. Allow to dry a little and then repeat until you have used about half of the glaze.

Place the ham on a trivet or wire rack in a shallow roasting pan and bake for 20 minutes or until the glaze starts to caramelise. Watch that the base of the pan doesn't start to burn; add a little water if necessary.

Working quickly, remove the ham from the oven and brush again with the glaze. Return to the oven for another 20 minutes or until the ham is beautifully glazed.

Let the ham cool to room temperature before carving and serving.

Roast Pork with Cumquat and Rosemary Stuffing

Pork has only become a favourite of mine in the last 10 years, since I came across the wonderful Colin and Joy Leinert of Sheoak Log in South Australia, who've been raising Berkshire pigs for 60 years (they're in their 80s now). The fat of the Berkshire pig is sweet, and I always choose a cut with a good layer of fat visible. Luckily, there are now a number of heritage breeds being farmed all over Australia and you'll be amazed at the superior flavour. Pork is a rich meat and, to me, there is no better accompaniment than the sharpness of cumquats (I get my dried cumquats from The Kumquatery, run by Noelle and Ian Tolley). Walnut breadcrumbs are made using walnut bread, but a good-quality sourdough will give an equally fine result.

SERVES 8

½ cup (125 ml) verjuice
1 × 1.2 kg boneless rolled pork loin (ask your butcher to score the skin and truss with cooking twine)
salt
vegetable oil (optional), for cooking
wilted cavolo nero or spinach, to serve

CUMQUAT AND ROSEMARY STUFFING

20 g unsalted butter
1 tablespoon extra virgin olive oil
1 onion, finely chopped
1½ tablespoons chopped rosemary
1 cup (70 g) walnut or sourdough breadcrumbs (see above)
5–6 dried cumquats, roughly chopped (to yield 50 g)
sea salt and freshly ground black pepper

Brush 2 tablespoons of the verjuice all over the pork loin, then rub 2 tablespoons salt into the skin. Set aside for 1 hour.

Meanwhile, to make the stuffing, melt the butter in a non-stick frying pan over high heat and cook for 3 minutes or until nut-brown, adding the olive oil when the butter starts to bubble to prevent it from burning. Add the onion and cook over medium heat for 8 minutes until light golden brown. Reduce the heat to low–medium, then add the rosemary and cook for a further 10 minutes or until burnished. Remove from the heat and stir in the breadcrumbs and cumquat, then season to taste with salt and pepper. Set aside to cool.

Preheat a fan-forced oven to 180°C (200°C).

Remove the cooking twine from the pork, then unroll the loin and place skin-side down on a chopping board. Spread the stuffing evenly over the pork flesh, leaving a 2 cm border, then re-roll the pork and truss with cooking twine again.

Place a wire rack or trivet in a shallow roasting pan, then place the pork loin on top. Roast the pork for 30 minutes, then reduce the oven temperature to 160°C fan-forced (180°C) and roast for a further 35 minutes or until the juices run a very pale pink when the loin is pierced with a skewer (if you have a meat thermometer, the internal temperature should register 64°C). Pour the remaining verjuice over the pork, cover loosely with foil and leave to rest for 30 minutes (the internal temperature should rise to 68°C in this time).

If crackling is important to you, heat some vegetable oil in the roasting pan over high heat until just starting to smoke and then gently and carefully spoon this hot oil over the crackling to crisp it.

Serve slices of the pork with wilted cavolo nero or spinach alongside.

Smoked Southern Herrings with Soba Noodles and Soy and Verjuice Dressing

I made this dish on a trip to Japan when we were introducing our verjuice into the market there. I was invited to cook on a very sophisticated version of a shopping channel, and I had to come up with dishes featuring my products that were relevant to the Japanese market. As ever, I learnt a lot along the way, most notably that the combination of soy sauce and verjuice is surprisingly good. It was a frightening experience though, cooking ten dishes while being filmed live, with an earpiece in each ear, one with instructions in English, the other in Japanese . . . one of the harder gigs of my television life, I can assure you – but, in retrospect at least, totally hilarious!

SERVES 4

½ cup (110 g) soft brown sugar
½ cup (110 g) caster sugar
50 g orange pekoe or green tea leaves
12 southern herring or sardine fillets, skin-on
180 g soba noodles

SOY AND VERJUICE DRESSING
2 teaspoons soy sauce
⅓ cup (80 ml) verjuice
¼ teaspoon white sugar
small handful finely chopped coriander leaves
100 ml extra virgin olive oil
¼ teaspoon sesame oil

Line the base of a wok (or flameproof roasting pan) with foil. Combine the brown sugar, caster sugar and tea leaves in a bowl, then tip into the wok or roasting pan.

Place an oiled wire rack that sits comfortably in the wok or dish about 5 cm above the tea mixture. Cover with a lid (or foil) to keep the smoke in. Place over high heat for 3–4 minutes (there will be a strong smell from the sugars caramelising). Reduce the heat to low and, working in batches if necessary, place the fish fillets skin-side down on the rack. Cover and smoke the fish for 5 minutes, then turn off the heat and leave for a further 3 minutes (if using foil, make sure it does not touch the fish).

Meanwhile, bring a large saucepan of water to the boil. Add the soba noodles, stirring so they don't stick together, and bring back to the boil. Cook for 4 minutes, then drain and run them under cold water to cool. Transfer to a bowl and set aside.

To make the dressing, place the soy sauce, verjuice, sugar and coriander in a bowl and whisk to dissolve the sugar. Slowly whisk in the oils until emulsified. Pour the dressing over the soba noodles and toss to coat well.

To serve, divide the noodles among four plates and top with the smoked fish fillets.

Rabbit with Braised Fennel Puree

Cooking rabbit is a labour of love for me; I think it's one of the hardest dishes to get right. Back in the early eighties, my great friend Stephanie Alexander taught me that each part of the rabbit needs to be cooked separately: the front legs, the back and the saddle. In those days we used wild rabbit; farmed rabbit is now readily available and is more forgiving, but even so, it has to be cooked with care.

SERVES 4

1.6 kg farmed rabbit with kidneys
sea salt
12 small pickling onions
2 rashers (40 g) traditionally smoked belly bacon, rind removed
40 g unsalted butter, plus extra if needed
2 tablespoons extra virgin olive oil, plus extra for drizzling
12 pitted prunes
2 tablespoons verjuice
1 cup (250 ml) Golden Chicken Stock (see page 190)

MARINADE

¼ cup (60 ml) extra virgin olive oil
1½ tablespoons verjuice
4 bay leaves
3 sprigs rosemary, leaves picked
small handful lemon thyme sprigs (strip leaves if sprigs are not soft)
sea salt

BRAISED FENNEL PUREE

350 g baby fennel bulbs (if unavailable, use 1 large fennel bulb), fronds trimmed and bulbs cut into 5 mm thick slices
½ cup (125 ml) extra virgin olive oil
1 cup (250 ml) verjuice
sea salt and freshly ground white pepper

To cut the rabbit into sections, remove the front legs and back legs. This will leave you with the saddle of the rabbit intact, with the kidneys encased in fat underneath. Using a flexible boning knife, remove the sinew from the saddle. Using a sharp heavy knife or cleaver, chop the saddle into three even pieces. Put the front and back legs and saddle pieces into a large bowl, then add the marinade ingredients and 2 teaspoons salt, cover with plastic film and leave to marinate for 1 hour at room temperature.

Meanwhile, to make the braised fennel puree, place the fennel, olive oil, verjuice and a good pinch of sea salt in a deep saucepan over high heat and bring to the boil. Immediately reduce the heat to low and cover with a lid. Gently simmer the fennel for 20–30 minutes or until cooked through and tender when pierced with a sharp knife. Drain the fennel, reserving the braising liquid, and place in a food processor or blender, then process to form a smooth puree; if the puree is very thick, add a small amount of the braising liquid. Adjust the seasoning with salt and pepper, then set aside.

Bring a saucepan of water to the boil and add a pinch of salt, then add the onions and boil for 15 minutes. Drain the onions, then set aside until cool enough to handle. Remove the outer layer of skin and set aside.

Preheat a fan-forced oven to 220°C (240°C).

Place a large heavy-based ovenproof frying pan over medium heat, drizzle in a little olive oil and add the bacon. Cook for 2 minutes on each side or until well coloured and beginning to crisp. Transfer to a plate and set aside.

Return the pan to medium heat, then add the butter and, as it melts and browns, add the olive oil. Add the rabbit and marinade, the prunes and reserved onions, then cook for a few minutes until the rabbit pieces are light golden on both sides, adding more butter if required.

Transfer the pan to the oven and cook for 10 minutes. Remove the front leg pieces to a warm plate, and continue to cook the remaining ingredients for 5–8 minutes.

Place the rabbit, onions and prunes on the warm plate and cover with foil. Return the frying pan to the stove over medium–high heat, then add the verjuice and cook, stirring and scraping the bottom of the pan, for 2–3 minutes. Add the bacon and stock to the pan and bring to a rapid boil over high heat, then simmer for 5–6 minutes or until the liquid has reduced by half. Return the rabbit, onions and prunes to the pan to warm through. Gently reheat the fennel puree.

Transfer to a large serving dish, then drizzle the sauce over and serve with a bowl of the braised fennel puree to the side.

Tripe with Leek, Peas and Belly Bacon

Tripe was the one food I couldn't stomach as a child, but all that changed on my first trip to Italy. I now love tripe and find the trick is to cook it until it is soft, then pat it dry before frying it in nut-brown butter until it's golden (much more appealing to me than milky white tripe!). The surprise here is the addition of dehydrated Surprise peas – they are intensely sweet and match beautifully with the leeks and the smoked bacon.

SERVES 4

---

300 g honeycomb tripe
40 g unsalted butter
extra virgin olive oil, for cooking
2 leeks, white part only, well washed and sliced into 1 cm thick rounds
1 tablespoon chopped thyme
½ cup (125 ml) verjuice
2 cups (500 ml) Golden Chicken Stock (see page 190)
sea salt
½ cup (60 g) dried Surprise peas
100 g traditionally smoked belly bacon, cut into 2 cm pieces
torn mint leaves, to serve

Place the tripe in a bowl and cover with cold water. Set aside for 30 minutes. Drain.

Bring a saucepan of water to the boil over high heat. Add the drained tripe and quickly return to the boil. Reduce the heat to medium and simmer the tripe for 20 minutes. Drain and leave to cool. Pat the tripe dry with paper towel, then cut into 2 cm pieces.

Melt the butter in a large saucepan over high heat and cook for 2 minutes or until nut-brown, adding a splash of olive oil when the butter starts to bubble to prevent it from burning. Reduce the heat to medium, then add the leek and cook for 10 minutes until softened. Stir in the thyme. Add the tripe and cook for 2 minutes on each side or until golden. Deglaze the pan with verjuice, scraping to remove any caught bits, then add the chicken stock and season with salt. Cover the pan with a tight-fitting lid and simmer gently for 1 hour.

Add the Surprise peas and cook for a further 25 minutes or until the peas are cooked through and the liquid is reduced and syrupy. Check the seasoning and adjust if necessary.

Meanwhile, heat a frying pan over medium–high heat, then dry-fry the bacon for 2 minutes on each side or until crisp. Transfer to a plate lined with paper towel to drain.

Scatter the tripe with torn mint leaves and the crisp bacon and serve.

Lamb Shanks with Dried Apricots, Green Peppercorns and Preserved Lemon

My mother used to roast lamb, probably the shoulder (but my memory is a little vague about that), with dried apricots – it's a magic combination to which I've added green peppercorns and preserved lemon. Long, slow cooking of lamb (or mutton for that matter), whether it's shanks, neck or shoulder, leaves the meat so tender it's almost melt-in-the-mouth. Best of all, it can be left to cook for hours and it's just the sort of dish that tastes even better the next day (refrigerate it overnight then remove the solidified fat before warming it up over very low heat). These flavours also work well with chicken thighs, braised and served with pasta.

SERVES 6

---

200 g dried apricots
¾ cup (180 ml) verjuice
¼ cup (60 ml) extra virgin olive oil, plus extra as required
6 × 400 g lamb shanks (ask your butcher to cut off the top knuckle and remove the sinew from the bone at the base; this is called 'French-trimming')
4 onions, roughly chopped
4 cloves garlic, sliced
3 tablespoons chopped rosemary
1 cup (250 ml) red wine
½ cup (125 ml) verjuice
¼ cup (60 ml) red wine vinegar
2 cups (500 ml) Golden Chicken Stock (see page 190)
2½ teaspoons tinned green peppercorns in brine, drained
4 preserved lemon quarters, flesh removed, rind rinsed and roughly chopped
sea salt and freshly ground black pepper

Soak the apricots in verjuice overnight (or for at least several hours). Alternatively, place the apricots and verjuice in a microwave-safe container and microwave on low for 2 minutes, then set aside for 20 minutes to reconstitute.

Preheat a fan-forced oven to 160°C (180°C).

Heat the olive oil in a large enamelled cast-iron (or other heavy-based) casserole over medium–high heat. Working in batches, add the shanks to the casserole and brown well on all sides. Transfer to a plate. Add the onion and a splash more oil to the pan, if needed, and cook for 5 minutes, stirring occasionally until softened, then add the garlic and rosemary and cook for a further 5 minutes. Add the wine, verjuice and vinegar and cook, stirring to scrape up any caught bits, for 1 minute. Return the lamb shanks to the pan, then add the stock and reserved verjuice.

Cover with a tight-fitting lid, bring to a simmer, then transfer to the oven and cook for 1 hour. Turn the shanks over, then cover and cook for a further 45 minutes. Turn the shanks again, scatter with the peppercorns, then add the apricots and their soaking liquid and the preserved lemon. Cover and cook for a further 30 minutes or until the meat is all but falling off the bone. Season to taste with salt and pepper.

Set the shanks and liquid aside to cool, then chill in the refrigerator until the fat has solidified on the surface. Remove the fat from the surface and discard. Transfer the shanks and apricots to a large plate, then bring the liquid to the boil over high heat. Reduce the heat to low and return the shanks and apricots to the pan, then simmer for 15 minutes or until heated through before serving.

Barbecued Quail with Vino Cotto and Verjuice Glaze

I love quail cooked on the bone at any time, whether it's poached, roasted, barbecued or grilled. However, the simple combination of vino cotto, extra virgin olive oil and fresh rosemary in this marinade gives an added dimension of flavour, not to mention a caramelised skin that looks spectacular for very little effort. This recipe calls for jumbo quail; if you're using standard quail (120–150 g each), you'll need to reduce the cooking time accordingly.

SERVES 8

8 x 200 g jumbo quail
⅓ cup (80 ml) vino cotto
⅓ cup (80 ml) extra virgin olive oil, plus extra for drizzling
4 bay leaves, crushed
2 large sprigs rosemary
2 tablespoons verjuice
1 quantity Salsa Agresto (see page 192), to serve

Using kitchen scissors, cut along either side of each quail backbone and remove. Open the quail out, skin-side up, and press down firmly with the heel of your hand to flatten.

Place the flattened quail in a large baking dish and drizzle with the vino cotto and olive oil. Add the bay leaves and rosemary and toss to coat the quail all over. Cover with plastic film and leave to marinate for 30 minutes, turning the quail over after 15 minutes and making sure all parts are in contact with the marinade.

Preheat a barbecue grill plate to high.

Place the quail, flesh-side down, on the hot grill plate. Cook the quail for 6 minutes, then turn and cook the skin-side for 2 minutes or until the meat is cooked through (as quail are so small I cook them for three-quarters of the cooking time on the flesh side). When it is ready, the leg meat should pull away easily. Transfer the quail to a plate and drizzle with the verjuice and extra oil. Cover loosely with foil and rest for 5 minutes.

Serve the quail with the resting juices spooned over and a bowl of salsa agresto alongside.

Tarragon Chicken Breasts with Grapes

Whenever I cook with chicken, I always use one of my daughter Saskia's Barossa chooks, of course, but any well-brought-up, free-range chicken (or chook, if you're my age) will make all the difference to the end result. Tarragon shares star billing here, but it must be French: the Russian variety won't impart the same flavour. This means it is a dish for spring and summer, when French tarragon is available.

SERVES 4

- 4 × 260 g chicken breast fillets from a Barossa or other well-brought-up chook, skin-on
- 2 tablespoons extra virgin olive oil, plus extra for drizzling
- sea salt
- 5 spring onions, trimmed and finely chopped
- 2 cloves garlic, roughly chopped
- ½ cup (125 ml) verjuice
- ½ cup (125 ml) Golden Chicken Stock (see page 190)
- handful shredded French tarragon
- ⅓ cup (80 ml) pure cream
- 1 teaspoon lemon thyme leaves
- 140 g green grapes, cut in half
- freshly ground white pepper

Place the chicken on a plate, drizzle with oil and season with salt, then leave to come to room temperature.

Heat the olive oil over medium heat in a large heavy-based frying pan with a tight-fitting lid that will fit the chicken snugly in one layer. Add the spring onion, then stir and cook for 1–2 minutes or until softened. Add the garlic and cook for a further 2 minutes.

Add the chicken to the pan, skin-side down, and cook over medium heat for 5 minutes or until the skin is golden brown. (If the spring onion and garlic start to burn, scrape from the pan and place on top of the chicken.) Turn the breasts over and cook for 4 minutes. Increase the heat to high, then add the verjuice and cook, stirring, until the verjuice has evaporated. Add the chicken stock, tarragon and cream, and cook until the liquid bubbles up. Season with salt, cover with the lid and cook for 2 minutes. Transfer the chicken to a plate and cover loosely with foil to keep it warm (the chicken will continue to cook while it rests).

Increase the heat, bring the remaining liquid to the boil and reduce by half. At the very last moment before serving, sprinkle in the thyme, add the grapes and season with salt and pepper.

Serve the chicken breasts immediately, with the sauce spooned around.

Eggplant and Lentil Stew with Pomegranate Molasses

The wonderful thing about this dish is that there is no need to pre-cook the eggplant: it's thrown in with the rest of the ingredients and everything is cooked together. It's a great dish for vegetarians, as I found when I was asked to present a vegetarian course as part of the dinner menu at the 2011 Noosa Food and Wine Festival. I cooked it in advance, then warmed it through at the last minute and served it scattered with fresh herbs and a final drizzle of oil. The easiest dish ever for a crowd, and so moreish it deserved its place alongside the more sophisticated dishes of the night.

SERVES 8

---

3 eggplants (aubergine), each cut into four lengthways
table salt, for sprinkling
1 cup (200 g) puy-style lentils
⅔ cup (160 ml) extra virgin olive oil
1 large onion, roughly chopped
5 cloves garlic, finely chopped
1 long green chilli, seeded and roughly chopped
sea salt
3 tomatoes, roughly chopped
½ cup (125 ml) verjuice
¼ teaspoon smoked paprika
¼ cup (70 g) pomegranate molasses
1 tablespoon rinsed and finely chopped preserved lemon rind
2 large handfuls flat-leaf parsley leaves, roughly chopped
large handful mint leaves, shredded

With a sharp knife, score the eggplant slices in a criss-cross pattern on both sides, then cut each slice crossways into four. Spread the pieces out on a tray lined with baking paper and sprinkle with salt. Leave for 1 hour, then rinse the salt off the eggplant and pat dry with paper towel.

Place the lentils and 1.5 litres water (do not add salt) in a saucepan over high heat and bring almost to the boil, then reduce the heat to low–medium and simmer for 15–18 minutes or until tender, making sure the water doesn't boil. Drain and set aside.

Preheat a fan-forced oven to 135°C (155°C).

Meanwhile, place a large enamelled cast-iron (or other heavy-based) casserole or saucepan over high heat and add ¼ cup (60 ml) of the oil. Once the oil is hot, add the onion and cook for 5 minutes or until golden brown, stirring occasionally. Add the garlic, chilli and a good pinch of salt and cook, stirring every now and then to prevent the onion from burning, for 3–4 minutes or until the onion is dark brown.

Stir in the tomato and another tablespoon of oil and cook for a minute or so before pouring in the verjuice. Cook, stirring, for 1 minute until the liquid has reduced by two-thirds, then remove from the heat and stir through the paprika. Add the eggplant, lentils, pomegranate molasses and remaining oil and gently stir to combine.

Cover and cook in the oven for 1 hour, then stir through the preserved lemon rind. Return to the oven for another 45 minutes–1 hour or until the eggplant has all but collapsed.

Check for seasoning and serve warm with the parsley and mint stirred through.

Slow-roasted Lamb Shoulder with Quince and Ginger Stuffing

Even when cooking meat slowly, the cooking time can vary greatly, depending on the cooking vessel, the strength of the oven and, of course, the cut of meat you use. Sometimes the difference can be as much as an hour or more. This beautifully tender lamb shoulder is wonderful served with a dish of soft, porridgy polenta. By the way, if the lamb comes rolled and enclosed in a net bag, you can stuff and cook it in this bag instead of using cooking twine to hold the shape.

SERVES 4–6

---

2 quinces
40 g unsalted butter
¼ cup (60 ml) extra virgin olive oil
1 tablespoon roughly chopped rosemary
2 onions, chopped
⅓ cup (80 ml) verjuice
1 × 5 cm piece fresh ginger, peeled and finely chopped
85 g coarse fresh breadcrumbs
finely grated zest of 1 lemon
5 sprigs lemon thyme or regular thyme, leaves picked
2 tablespoons roughly chopped flat-leaf parsley leaves
sea salt and freshly ground black pepper
1 × 1 kg lamb shoulder, boned

VERJUICE BASTING MIX
2 tablespoons verjuice
2 tablespoons extra virgin olive oil
sea salt and freshly ground black pepper

Bring a saucepan of water to the boil, pop the whole quinces in, then cover and cook for 20 minutes or until the flesh is tender when pierced with a skewer. Remove from the water and, when cool enough to handle, trim the ends, carefully peel away the skin and cut the flesh into quarters (or sixths if the quinces are large). Cut away the core, roughly chop the flesh and set aside.

Melt half the butter in a non-stick frying pan over high heat for 2 minutes or until nut-brown, adding a tablespoon of the oil when the butter starts to bubble to prevent it from burning. Add the rosemary and onion and cook for 5 minutes or until the onion is golden and well caramelised, then transfer to a mixing bowl.

Place the pan back on the stove over medium–high heat and add the remaining butter and a tablespoon of the olive oil. Once the butter has melted, add the reserved quince and cook for 3–4 minutes or until golden, then pour in half the verjuice and cook, stirring, for about 20 seconds or until syrupy. Stir in the ginger and continue to cook for a further 2 minutes, then turn off the heat and transfer to the mixing bowl, along with the breadcrumbs, lemon zest, thyme, parsley and 1 teaspoon salt. Season to taste with pepper, then combine until the stuffing just holds together.

Preheat a fan-forced oven to 120°C (140°C).

Open out the boned shoulder on a chopping board, skin-side down. Spread the stuffing over the lamb, roll up and secure with cooking twine. Season well on all sides.

Heat the remaining oil in an enamelled cast-iron (or other heavy-based) casserole over medium heat. Brown the lamb for 10 minutes or until coloured on all sides. Pour in the remaining verjuice and cook, stirring, for a minute or two to reduce. Place the lid on and transfer the casserole to the oven to cook for 2½ hours, then remove and turn the meat over.

To make the verjuice basting mix, combine all the ingredients in a small bowl. Pour over the lamb and return to the oven for 1–2 hours or until the meat is absolutely fall-apart tender.

Remove the meat from the casserole and set aside to rest for at least 30 minutes.

Carve into slices and serve with plenty of cooking juices spooned over.

Pork, Verjuice and Fennel Sausages

It's really good fun to make your own sausages, especially when you've got plenty of willing helpers and an electric mixer with a sausage attachment. Use the best-quality pork mince you can find, and don't stint on the fat ratio as it makes all the difference to the flavour and texture. Make sure all the ingredients are super-cold before you begin as it helps them to bind together. And please – don't be tempted to prick the sausages and let all that precious fat out of them! What could be better to serve these with than some mashed potato and a salad of bitter greens . . .

MAKES 10

2½ teaspoons fennel seeds
700 g coarsely minced pork shoulder
300 g coarsely minced pork fat
3 teaspoons sea salt
1 teaspoon freshly ground black pepper
1 clove garlic, minced or crushed
1½ teaspoons thyme leaves
½ cup (125 ml) white wine
½ cup (125 ml) verjuice
1 × 1½ metre large sausage casing, rinsed
2 tablespoons extra virgin olive oil

Place a small non-stick frying pan over medium–high heat and dry-fry the fennel seeds, tossing occasionally, for 3–4 minutes or until lightly coloured and aromatic. Remove and bruise lightly with a mortar and pestle, then set aside to cool.

Place the minced pork and fat, salt, pepper, garlic, thyme and cooled fennel seeds in a large mixing bowl. Using your hands, combine the mixture well, gathering it together in a ball and slapping it against the side of the bowl a few times until firm and sticky. Cover with plastic film and refrigerate for 2 hours to let the flavours infuse.

Transfer the sausage mix to an electric mixer fitted with the paddle attachment. Switch on to low speed and, with the motor running, slowly pour in the white wine and verjuice and mix until incorporated. Turn the speed up to high and mix for another 30 seconds.

Feed one end of the sausage casing over the end of the sausage nozzle attachment on your mixer (or over the nozzle of a piping bag). With wet hands, tie a knot in the end of the casing. If using a sausage nozzle attachment, feed the sausage mix through the food grinder with the motor running and fill the casing with the mixture, tying a knot at the open end of the casing once filled.

If using a piping bag, fill the bag with sausage mix and squeeze to fill the casing, working in batches if necessary. Tie a knot at the open end of the casing once filled.

Twist the casing tightly at 10 cm intervals, then transfer to a large plate (refrigerate if not cooking straightaway).

Heat the oil in a non-stick frying pan over low–medium heat and cook the sausages for 10–12 minutes, turning every couple of minutes so you get an even colour. Remove the sausages from the pan and leave them to rest on a plate for 5 minutes before serving.

Pasta with Smoked Trout and Salmon Roe

This classic dish from the Pheasant Farm days has morphed over time into something much lighter than the original. How many times would Colin entreat me over the years to make it, but I always resisted, citing the fact that there was far too much cream in it. I blanch at the fact that I probably used as much cream as fish stock when I cooked it in those days, but it was the eighties after all. Recently, my daughter Saskia and I were asked to present a dinner at Thredbo and, as they had locally smoked trout, she made this much lighter version. I was reminded that the essence of the dish deserved another life. If you can't find a beautifully moist, pink smoked trout, then look for a smoked ocean trout fillet, like the ones from Harris Smokehouse in Hahndorf. I use Yarra Valley salmon roe, which is both beautifully flavoursome and sustainable, as the roe is hand-milked before the fish is released back into the water.

SERVES 4

---

extra virgin olive oil, for cooking and drizzling
6 strands saffron
1 golden shallot, finely sliced
3 stalks flat-leaf parsley
1 cup (250 ml) verjuice
3 cups (750 ml) Fish Stock (see page 191)
2 teaspoons Pernod
1 tablespoon pure cream
120 g cold unsalted butter, diced
sea salt and freshly ground white pepper
280 g smoked trout fillet, flaked
400 g spaghettini or linguine
2 tablespoons salmon roe
2 tablespoons finely chopped chives, dill or chervil (depending on what's in season)
freshly ground black pepper

Heat a splash of olive oil in a saucepan over medium heat. Add the saffron, shallot and parsley stalks and saute for 5 minutes or until the shallot is soft. Add the verjuice, then increase the heat to high and cook, stirring, for 15 minutes or until the liquid has reduced to about 2 tablespoons. Strain into a clean frying pan and set aside, discarding the solids.

Simmer the fish stock in a saucepan over high heat for 10–12 minutes or until reduced by a third, then add the Pernod and remove from the heat. Cover and keep warm.

Heat the reserved cooking liquid in a frying pan over low heat. When warmed through, stir in the cream with a wooden spoon, then, working in batches and stirring between each addition, add the chopped butter a cube at a time. (You may need to remove the pan from the heat now and again while adding the butter to make sure the sauce does not boil.) Season, then stir in the warm stock mixture, add the smoked trout and cook for 1 minute just to warm through, then remove the pan from the heat.

Meanwhile, cook the pasta in a large saucepan of boiling salted water following the instructions on the packet, then drain and transfer to a bowl. Drizzle with oil to moisten.

Gently fold the sauce through the pasta and divide among warmed bowls. Top each with 2 teaspoons of the salmon roe, scatter over the herbs and finish with a grind or two of black pepper.

Poussins with Pomegranate, Blood Orange and Belly Bacon

We have between 150 and 200 pomegranate bushes at home and I love to use the pomegranate seeds in salads or crush them to make pomegranate juice. Whilst their season is very much autumn, I am so partial to the flavour of pomegranate that I always have some pomegranate molasses on hand in the pantry to use during the rest of the year. The bold flavours of the pomegranate, blood orange and belly bacon really lift this dish. I do love serving one-pot dishes like this in winter, just plonked down in the middle of the table with a bowl of soft polenta and a salad of bitter leaves.

SERVES 4

40 g unsalted butter
extra virgin olive oil, for cooking
8 golden shallots, peeled and halved lengthways
2 sprigs rosemary
1 sprig thyme
2 bay leaves
zest of 1 orange (use blood orange, if available), removed in thin strips with a vegetable peeler, leaving the bitter pith, flesh reserved for salad (if making)
2 × 400 g poussins (baby chickens)
sea salt and freshly ground black pepper
2 teaspoons pomegranate molasses
¼ cup (60 ml) verjuice
3 rashers (60 g) traditionally smoked belly bacon, cut into 1 cm pieces
¾ cup (180 ml) Golden Chicken Stock (see page 190)

BLOOD ORANGE, ROCKET AND POMEGRANATE SALAD (OPTIONAL)

½ cup (50 g) walnuts
1 pomegranate, broken open and seeds released without pith
flesh from 1 orange (from above recipe), pith removed, sliced
1 tablespoon mint leaves
sea salt and freshly ground black pepper
1 bunch rocket, leaves picked, washed and dried
extra virgin olive oil

Melt the butter in a large heavy-based frying pan over low–medium heat and cook for 2 minutes until nut-brown, adding a splash of oil when the butter starts to bubble to prevent it from burning. Stir in the shallot, rosemary, thyme, bay leaves and orange zest to coat in the butter mixture, then push to the side of the pan. Add the poussins, then lightly sprinkle with salt and cook over low heat for 10 minutes, turning until each side is light golden. Add the pomegranate molasses and cook for 5 minutes, turning the poussins until all sides are coated and the skin becomes burnished.

Increase the heat to medium, then add the verjuice and cook, stirring, for 1 minute. Add the belly bacon and stock and cover the pan with a tight-fitting lid. Bring to a gentle simmer and cook for 5 minutes, then remove the lid and cook for another 15 minutes. Turn the heat off, then leave the poussins to rest in the pan for another 10–15 minutes; they should be just cooked through.

If making the salad, preheat a fan-forced oven to 200°C (220°C). Place the walnuts on a baking tray and roast for 5 minutes or until golden, checking them frequently to make sure they don't burn. Immediately wrap in a clean tea towel and rub to remove the skins. Shake the walnuts in a sieve to get rid of the skins, then set aside to cool.

Mix the pomegranate seeds with the orange flesh, then add the mint and nuts, season to taste with salt and pepper and toss with the rocket and a splash of olive oil.

Cut each poussin in half using kitchen scissors and serve with the juices from the pan, with the salad alongside, if using.

Pot-roasted Pickled Pork Shoulder with Flo Beer's Pickled Quince

This is a sentimental dish for me. My late mother-in-law Flo cooked this for me the first time I met the family, and that was the day I fell in love with pickled pork and quinces (it was the first time I'd ever tasted quince). The secret to getting the deep, rich colour and flavour of the pork is to use a really heavy enamelled cast-iron casserole. As to the quinces, they'll gradually attain a rosy glow as they cook, but will only develop the deep ruby-red colour over time in the jar (they'll need to mature for several weeks before using). Cook them at just a simmer until soft; don't overcook them in an attempt to colour them as they will lose their shape.

SERVES 8–10

¼ cup (60 ml) extra virgin olive oil
1 × 2.3 kg whole boned pickled pork shoulder (ask your butcher to truss with cooking twine)
10 golden shallots, peeled
sea salt and freshly ground black pepper
½ cup (125 ml) verjuice
½ cup (125 ml) Golden Chicken Stock (see page 190)
4 bay leaves
zest of 1 orange, removed in thin strips with a vegetable peeler, leaving the bitter pith
2 star anise
2 tablespoons soft brown sugar
Dijon mustard, to serve

FLO BEER'S PICKLED QUINCE
1 kg quinces
juice of ½ lemon
3 cups (750 ml) white wine vinegar
375 g caster sugar
3 teaspoons cloves
1 tablespoon black peppercorns

To prepare the pickled quinces, wash, peel and core the quinces, then cut into quarters or sixths (depending on the size), retaining the skins and cores. Put the cut quinces immediately into a bowl of water with lemon juice added to prevent discolouration.

Wrap and tie the reserved skins and cores in a piece of muslin. Place the vinegar, sugar, spices and muslin bag in a large heavy-based saucepan over high heat and cook for 10 minutes or until a thin syrup begins to form. Remove the muslin bag, then add the quince wedges to the pan and place the muslin bag back on top. Simmer over low heat for 20–40 minutes or until the quince starts to turn pink.

Remove the muslin bag then, using a slotted spoon, transfer the quinces to clean, dry jars. When each jar is almost full, bring the syrup back to the boil, then transfer to a heatproof jug and pour into each of the jars to cover the quinces. Seal the jars, then invert and leave to cool completely. (The colour of the quince will deepen in the jar over time.)

Preheat a fan-forced oven to 140°C (160°C).

Heat the oil over medium–high heat in an enamelled cast-iron (or other heavy-based) casserole large enough to just fit the pork snugly. Add the pork and shallots, then cook for 10 minutes, turning to seal the pork on all sides and tossing the shallots in the oil. Season lightly with salt and pepper. Add the verjuice, chicken stock, bay leaves, orange zest, star anise and brown sugar, stirring to spread the ingredients evenly around the base of the pan. Cover with a tight-fitting lid and roast for 1 hour.

Remove the lid and return to the oven to cook for a further 50 minutes–1 hour or until the juices run clear when the pork is pierced with a skewer (if you have a meat thermometer, the internal temperature should register 64°C); the pork will caramelise and brown on the top and the juices will become syrupy.

Remove the casserole from the oven and leave the pork to rest with the lid on for 10 minutes. If you have a meat thermometer, test the pork now: the internal temperature should register 68°C. Rest the pork in the juices for another 30 minutes.

Serve slices of the pork either warm, at room temperature or chilled with pickled quinces and Dijon mustard alongside.

Salmon with Verjuice Beurre Blanc

I love the flavour of a beurre blanc made with verjuice: it's quite different to that of the classic made with white wine and/or vinegar. Using verjuice, by some sort of strange kitchen chemistry, allows you to add the butter to the reduction in large batches, rather than bit by bit, making it a much quicker process. You could of course use ocean trout here in place of salmon.

SERVES 4

4 × 140 g salmon fillets, skin-on and pin-boned
sea salt
2 tablespoons extra virgin olive oil
2 teaspoons unsalted butter
juice of 1 lemon
1 teaspoon chopped chervil *or* 1 tablespoon snipped chives (optional)
steamed green vegetables, to serve

VERJUICE BEURRE BLANC
2 golden shallots, thinly sliced
1 cup (250 ml) verjuice
sea salt
1 tablespoon pure cream
180 g chilled unsalted butter, chopped
freshly ground white pepper

To make the beurre blanc, place the shallot, verjuice and a small pinch of salt in a small saucepan over medium heat. Simmer until the liquid has reduced to about 2 tablespoons and is syrupy. Keep warm. Strain and remove the shallot if desired (I usually keep it as part of the sauce). Add the cream to the pan, then add one-quarter of the butter at a time, whisking constantly to emulsify it with the reduced verjuice and taking the pan on and off the heat without allowing the sauce to boil, until all the butter is incorporated; the sauce should be thick enough to coat the back of a wooden spoon. Season to taste with salt and white pepper. (If making in advance, pour the hot sauce into a wide-mouthed thermos flask and seal until required.)

Heat a large frying pan over medium–high heat until hot. Season the skin of the salmon with salt.

Add the olive oil to the pan and place the salmon, skin-side down, in the pan. Cook for 2 minutes or until the skin is crisp and you can see that the fillets are cooked halfway up their thickness. Working quickly, transfer the salmon to a warm plate.

Using paper towel, wipe the pan clean and then add the butter; the pan will still be hot and the butter will melt quickly. Place the pan over low heat. Season the flesh-side of the salmon with salt, then place it flesh-side down in the pan and cook for no more than 1 minute.

Remove the pan from the heat and leave the salmon in the pan; the centre of the fish should be only just 'set'.

Transfer the fish to serving plates and scatter over the chervil or chives, if using. Serve with the verjuice beurre blanc and some steamed green vegetables alongside.

Maggie's Perfect Roast Chicken with Hazelnut and Herb Stuffing

I cooked this chook, albeit without this lovely stuffing, as part of a masterclass for an episode of *MasterChef Australia*, when four contestants came to see me in the Barossa Valley. I've never, ever had so many comments on a dish. For three weeks after the show aired, not only did I receive a deluge of emails, but everywhere I went I was pulled up to be told about the 'hallelujah' moment so many people had as they watched. They were so anxious to let me know they had never tasted a chook as good, and that they had got the message about the importance of using a well-brought-up bird, as well as the other small details involved (see page 136).

SERVES 8

---

1 × 2 kg Barossa or other well-brought-up chook
lemon juice, to taste
⅓ cup (80 ml) extra virgin olive oil
sea salt
100 ml verjuice
handful thyme sprigs, to serve
roasted vegetables, to serve

HAZELNUT AND HERB STUFFING
¼ cup (35 g) hazelnuts
2 rashers (40 g) traditionally smoked belly bacon
2 chicken livers, rinsed
¼ cup (60 ml) extra virgin olive oil, plus extra if needed
2 onions, finely chopped
small handful rosemary leaves
small handful thyme leaves
2 cloves garlic, finely chopped
1 cup (70 g) fresh breadcrumbs
¼ cup (40 g) dried cherries or cranberries

To prepare the stuffing, preheat a fan-forced oven to 180°C (200°C).

Place the hazelnuts on a baking tray and roast for 8 minutes or until golden, checking them frequently to make sure they don't burn. Immediately wrap in a clean tea towel and rub to remove the skins. Shake the hazelnuts in a sieve to get rid of the skins, then set aside to cool. Roughly chop.

Heat a non-stick frying pan over high heat, then add the bacon and cook for 1 minute, tossing occasionally. Transfer to a plate and roughly chop when cooled. Add the chicken livers to the pan and cook for 30–45 seconds on each side or until lightly browned. Transfer to a plate and leave to rest for 5 minutes, then remove and discard any sinew and chop into small chunks.

Wipe out the pan, pour in the oil and place over medium heat. Add the onion and cook for 10 minutes or until golden, stirring occasionally. Add the rosemary and thyme and cook for just a minute, then transfer the mixture to a bowl. Stir in the garlic, breadcrumbs, cherries and chopped hazelnuts, mixing well, then add the liver and bacon and gently stir to just combine. Add some extra oil if necessary to bind the mixture, then set aside to cool.

Preheat a fan-forced oven to 200°C (220°C).

Wipe the skin of the chook and the inside cavity with paper towel. Squeeze a generous amount of lemon juice into the cavity, then fill the cavity with the cooled stuffing. Rub the chook all over with half the olive oil and the salt.

Place a trivet or a wire rack in a shallow roasting pan. Fold the wing tips under the bird and place on the rack, breast-side up. Cover the breast loosely with foil to prevent it drying out, then roast for 40 minutes.

CONTINUED >

Remove the chook from the oven and take off the foil. Brush the breast with the remaining oil and drizzle over ⅓ cup (80 ml) of the verjuice. Add a little water to the pan to prevent the verjuice from burning. Reduce the oven temperature to 180°C fan-forced (200°C), then return the chook to the oven and cook for a further 30 minutes. Check by inserting a skewer through the thickest part of the thigh joint to make sure the juices run clear. If there are any signs of pinkness, return the chook to the oven. Just be careful not to overcook it, as it will continue to cook during the resting time.

Remove the chook from the oven and turn it over in the pan so that it is breast-side down. Leave it to rest, covered loosely with foil, in the roasting juices for at least 20 minutes before carving.

While the bird is resting, skim away the fat from the roasting pan with a spoon and discard. Pour the remaining juices through a small fine-meshed sieve into a small saucepan and warm over low heat, adding the remaining verjuice to taste. Simmer over low heat for a few minutes to reduce and thicken, then transfer the gravy to a jug.

For added effect (and flavour), insert a handful of thyme sprigs into the cavity of the cooked chook. Serve on a large plate accompanied by a bowl of roasted vegetables and the gravy.

MY TIPS FOR THE PERFECT ROAST CHOOK

- If you have the time, make the stuffing the night before, and store it in a cool place (don't refrigerate it unless you live in a hot, humid climate, in which case the fridge is best).
- Make your own breadcrumbs for the stuffing ideally from good-quality bread such as sourdough.
- Make sure you bring the bird to room temperature before cooking. In temperate climes, this means taking it out of the fridge between 30 minutes and 2 hours before cooking; in hot, humid conditions, between 10–15 minutes should do it, but always err on the side of caution when dealing with uncooked poultry.
- Always turn the wings so the tips sit under the bird: this will help the breast cook more evenly.
- Cook in a preheated oven and make sure that the oven rack is at the right level for the size of the bird.
- Roast the chook breast-side up to start with and cover the breast with foil to prevent it drying out. With time, this step may not be necessary as experience will tell you when the chook is ready and you'll be less likely to overcook it.
- Always rest the chook breast-side down for at least 20 minutes after cooking. Don't skimp on the resting time: a well-rested chook served at room temperature will be infinitely more moist and flavoursome than one that has been served immediately after cooking.
- If you have a meat thermometer, test the temperature 10 minutes into the resting time by inserting it into the thickest part of the thigh joint: a perfectly cooked chicken will be 65–68°C.

Middle Eastern Chicken and Rice

I first tasted this dish when I was a guest of an Armenian/Lebanese family, the Oskey's, for lunch. In truth, it was a feast as, one after the other, dishes were brought out of the small kitchen, and we devoured every last bit. I particularly loved this chicken dish, and since then it's become one I make often, with a few of my own embellishments added. It's a dish I like to eat warm rather than hot, but you do need to work quickly so the shredded chicken breast doesn't get cold (you could warm it up quickly in the microwave if this happens).

SERVES 6

½ cup (40 g) flaked almonds
⅓ cup (55 g) dried currants
1 cup (250 ml) verjuice
1 × 1.6 kg Barossa or other well-brought-up chook, skin-on, cut into six pieces (ask your butcher to do this for you)
1 cinnamon stick
sea salt
20 g unsalted butter
¼ cup (60 ml) extra virgin olive oil
1 clove garlic, finely chopped
freshly ground black pepper
½ teaspoon ground cinnamon, plus extra to garnish
¼ teaspoon ground allspice
1¼ cups (250 g) brown rice, washed and drained
2 preserved lemon quarters, flesh removed, rind rinsed and finely chopped
handful flat-leaf parsley leaves, roughly chopped

Preheat a fan-forced oven to 200°C (220°C).

Place the almonds on a baking tray and roast for 5–8 minutes or until golden, checking them frequently to make sure they don't burn. Remove and set aside to cool.

Place the currants and ⅓ cup (80 ml) of the verjuice in a small saucepan and bring almost to the boil over high heat. Remove from the heat and set aside to steep for 30 minutes, then drain, reserving the soaking liquid.

Place the chicken pieces in a large stockpot and cover with 1.5 litres water and the remaining verjuice. Add the cinnamon stick and 2 teaspoons salt and bring to the boil, then reduce the heat to low and simmer, covered, for 30 minutes or until the meat is cooked through and tender. Drain the chicken pieces, reserving the stock, then set them aside to rest, loosely covered with foil.

Rinse out the stockpot and place over medium heat. Add the butter and olive oil and, when hot, add the garlic and cook for 2 minutes, taking care it does not burn. Measure 2 cups (500 ml) of the reserved stock and add this to the pot, along with the reserved soaking liquid, spices, ½ teaspoon black pepper and the brown rice. Bring to just below boiling point, then reduce the heat to low, cover and cook for 1 hour or until the rice is just cooked through.

When the chicken pieces are cool enough to handle, transfer them to a chopping board. Remove the meat from the bones and shred, discarding the skin. Place the shredded meat back in the pot, along with the preserved lemon, parsley, reserved currants and almonds, then stir through and season to taste.

END

Rhubarb and Apple Crumble

I love a rhubarb crumble and, depending on the season, I like to add sliced apple, quince or pear to complement the rhubarb. When pairing with apples, I tend to use Granny Smiths because I love their tartness, or Pink Ladies if they are in season, as their flavour really shines through in the cooking. Runny cream is a must with crumble, but a great-quality vanilla ice cream wouldn't go amiss either.

SERVES 4–6

¼ cup (55 g) soft brown sugar
¼ cup (60 ml) verjuice
50 g unsalted butter, melted, plus 20 g extra, chopped
6 Granny Smith apples, peeled and cored
20 sticks rhubarb, washed, trimmed and cut into 3 cm lengths
cream or ice cream, to serve

CRUMBLE MIXTURE
1 cup (150 g) plain flour
½ cup (110 g) soft brown sugar
1 cup (90 g) rolled oats
1 teaspoon ground cinnamon
1 teaspoon ground ginger
60 g unsalted butter, chopped

Preheat a fan-forced oven to 180°C (200°C).

For the crumble mixture, combine the flour, sugar, oats and spices in a large bowl. Rub the butter into the dry ingredients until the mixture resembles coarse breadcrumbs. Set aside.

Combine the sugar, verjuice and melted butter in a bowl. Cut the apple into very thin slices and add to the verjuice mixture, tossing to combine well. Transfer to a 2 litre baking dish (mine is 33 cm × 18 cm × 5 cm) and spread out evenly. Scatter the rhubarb over the apple.

Bake the apple and rhubarb mixture for 20 minutes. Spread the crumble mixture evenly over the top and dot with the extra chopped butter; don't press down too much or the crumble will become soggy. Bake for a further 30–35 minutes or until the fruit mixture bubbles around the edges and the crumble is nicely browned.

Spoon out at the table and serve with cream or ice cream.

Creme Caramel with Cinnamon, Lemon and Grapes

Recently, I wanted to cook the creme caramel I used to make in the Pheasant Farm days, but of course I'd never recorded the recipe (in all the years of the restaurant, only a handful of recipe cards written by apprentices were ever kept). Thankfully, my friend (and former apprentice) Sophie Zalokar had kept this one, so I was able to tinker with it to create this more 'grown-up' version, with its influences of cinnamon, lemon and grapes. What is the same is the dark caramel, with its slightly bitter edge – pale caramels are too sweet for my palate. I use an ovenproof mould with angled sides (12 cm in diameter at the base and 16 cm in diameter across the top), but a straight-sided one will work just as well. If you want to serve this turned out (as pictured here), it's better to make it the day before, keep it in the fridge and turn it out just before serving. Or, you can do as we do and eat it straight from the dish as soon as it has cooled.

SERVES 4

280 ml milk
140 ml pure cream
1 cinnamon stick
2 strips lemon zest, removed with a vegetable peeler, leaving the bitter pith
3 eggs
⅓ cup (75 g) caster sugar
boiling water, to cover
200 g red seedless grapes, cut in half

CARAMEL
1 cup (220 g) caster sugar
1 cup (250 ml) verjuice

Place the milk, cream, cinnamon stick and lemon zest in a saucepan over medium–high heat, bring almost to the boil, then reduce the heat to low–medium and simmer for 5 minutes. Remove from the heat and set aside for 1 hour to allow the flavours to infuse, then strain into a jug.

Meanwhile, to make the caramel, place the sugar and verjuice in a saucepan along with 1 cup (250 ml) water and bring to the boil over high heat. Cook for 10–15 minutes or until the mixture reduces and turns a dark caramel colour, stirring to dissolve the sugar and brushing down the sides of the pan now and then. Transfer immediately to a heatproof jug and leave to cool. When cold, pour half the mixture into a 600 ml ovenproof mould, reserving the rest. Set the mould on top of a folded Chux (J-cloth) in a large roasting tin.

Preheat a fan-forced oven to 160°C (180°C).

In a bowl, lightly whisk the eggs and sugar together until combined, then pour in the strained milk, whisking continuously. Pour the custard through a sieve into the caramel-lined mould, filling it to the top; reserve the lemon zest from the sieve. Use a spoon to skim off any bubbles that form on the surface of the custard.

Pour enough boiling water into the roasting tin to come two-thirds of the way up the sides of the mould, then carefully transfer to the oven and cook for 50 minutes or until the custard is set but still slightly wobbly (the cooking time will vary depending on the type of dish you use and your oven; if you have a 'hot' oven you may need to lower the temperature slightly or cook it for less time). Remove from the oven and leave to cool in the water bath. If serving the next day, cover and refrigerate, then turn out just before serving.

To serve, toss the halved grapes and the reserved lemon zest through the remaining caramel and pour over the top.

Chestnut Panna Cotta and Verjuice-poached Pears with Chocolate and Vino Cotto Sauce

How I love that silky feel panna cotta has when it's made with just enough gelatine to set it so it still has that delightful wobble as you bring it to the table. Making your own chestnut puree in late autumn or early winter is great – but I won't lie, it's a big job, so I consider buying a tin of unsweetened chestnut puree to be far from cheating. I've found the quality of the French brand I buy excellent as it's milled so finely that it's perfect for desserts. Chestnut is a very rich flavour and whilst most cooks find chocolate a natural partner to it, I find I need the piquancy of the vino cotto (cooked grape must) as well.

SERVES 10

800 ml pure cream
¾ cup (180 ml) milk
200 g unsweetened chestnut puree
2½ x 2 g gold-strength gelatine leaves
1 cup (220 g) caster sugar
1 cup (250 ml) verjuice
1 cinnamon stick
zest of 1 orange, removed in thin strips with a vegetable peeler, leaving the bitter pith
6 corella pears, thinly sliced lengthways

CHOCOLATE AND VINO COTTO SAUCE

55 g dark chocolate, chopped
2 tablespoons thickened cream
40 g caster sugar
1 teaspoon vino cotto

Bring the cream, milk and chestnut puree just to a boil in a saucepan and then immediately remove from the heat. Blend with a stick blender to combine, then set aside.

Soften the gelatine leaves in water for 3–4 minutes, then squeeze to remove excess moisture. Stir through the milk mixture until dissolved. Strain through a fine-meshed sieve into a jug, then leave to cool to room temperature. Divide among ten 125 ml dariole moulds. Cover and refrigerate for 4 hours or until set.

Place the sugar, 200 ml of the verjuice, the cinnamon, orange zest and 1 cup (250 ml) water in a large, heavy-based saucepan and bring to a boil. Reduce the heat to medium and cook, stirring, for 5–6 minutes or until light golden and a little syrupy, then remove from the heat. Stir in the remaining verjuice and the pear slices. Return the pan to the stove and cook over low heat for 5 minutes or until the pear is soft but not breaking up, then remove the pear with a slotted spoon. Cook the verjuice mixture for a further 3–5 minutes or until reduced to a syrupy consistency, then reserve.

Place a non-stick frying pan over medium heat, add the pear slices and dry-fry them on each side for 2–3 minutes or until golden brown.

To make the sauce, place the chocolate in a mixing bowl. Bring the cream to a boil in a small saucepan over high heat, then remove from the heat and immediately pour over the chocolate. Set aside for 2 minutes, then gently swirl the bowl to amalgamate the melted chocolate with the cream.

In another saucepan, combine the sugar with 1 tablespoon water over high heat, stirring until the sugar has dissolved. Remove from the heat and whisk into the chocolate mix to combine, then stir in the vino cotto. Set aside to cool.

When ready to serve, unmould the panna cotta by dipping them briefly in hot water and turning out onto individual plates. Serve with the verjuice-poached pears, a little syrup, some orange zest and the chocolate and vino cotto sauce.

Fruit Mince in Verjuice Syrup with Ice Cream

This is one of those recipes that came about simply by chance. One year I had a whole pile of beautiful South Australian dried fruits left over from making Christmas puddings, so I thought I'd try just putting them all together in a pan with some sherry, verjuice and spices, then make a verjuice sugar syrup to stir through at the end. It's a variation of a classic fruit mince and you could substitute your own favourite dried fruits (for instance, I don't like glace cherries, but you could easily add them). This can be used as a filling for mince pies; just make sure you drain off the syrup or the pastry will be soggy. This recipe makes more than you'll need, and the leftovers can be kept in a sealed jar in the refrigerator for those moments when you want something sweet after dinner. It'll last for weeks, but I bet it doesn't!

SERVES 4–6

---

3 small Granny Smith apples, unpeeled, cored and coarsely grated
100 g candied mixed peel
100 g sultanas
100 g raisins
100 g soft brown sugar
½ cup (125 ml) sweet sherry
200 ml verjuice
¼ teaspoon ground nutmeg
¼ teaspoon ground cloves
¼ teaspoon ground cinnamon
100 g candied orange pieces, roughly chopped
vanilla ice cream, to serve

VERJUICE SYRUP
1 cup (250 ml) verjuice
1 cup (220 g) soft brown sugar

Place the apple, mixed peel, sultanas, raisins, sugar, sherry, verjuice, nutmeg, cloves and cinnamon in a heavy-based saucepan over medium heat and bring to a simmer. Cook for 20–25 minutes or until almost all of the liquid has evaporated. Stir in the candied orange. Set aside for 30–40 minutes or until cooled to room temperature.

For the verjuice syrup, place the verjuice and brown sugar in a saucepan over low heat and bring to a simmer, stirring to dissolve the sugar. Simmer for 10–15 minutes or until the syrup has thickened and reduced to ½ cup (125 ml). Set aside to cool.

Stir the cooled verjuice syrup through the cooled fruit mince. Place a generous scoop of ice cream in deep plates or bowls, then spoon over about 2 tablespoons of the fruit mince mixture and serve at once.

Buckwheat and Almond Cake with Honey-and-verjuice-poached Persimmons

My friend and former apprentice Sophie Zalokar and her husband Chris live in Western Australia, where they run a cooking school with self-contained accommodation called Foragers. She has found her niche in the beautiful countryside around Pemberton, with wild marron and truffles on her doorstep. Sophie grew up cooking with verjuice and after four years working alongside me, she wasn't hard-pressed when I asked her to find a verjuice recipe to include in this book! The persimmons used here are the modern, non-astringent variety (although I must say there's nothing I love more than the old-fashioned persimmon that can't be eaten until its skin is see-through and the fruit has almost collapsed with ripeness).

SERVES 8

2 cups (160 g) flaked almonds
170 g unsalted butter, softened
180 g caster sugar
6 eggs, separated
1 teaspoon vanilla extract
table salt
130 g buckwheat flour
icing sugar (optional), for dusting
double cream, to serve

HONEY-AND-VERJUICE-POACHED PERSIMMONS

220 g Karri honey (if unavailable, use Jarrah or Leatherwood)
2 cups (500 ml) verjuice
½ vanilla bean, split
zest and juice of 1 orange, zest removed in thin strips with a vegetable peeler, leaving the bitter pith
3 large ripe Fuyu or other non-astringent persimmons, calyx removed, peeled and cut into 5 mm thick slices

For the honey-and-verjuice-poached persimmons, place the honey, verjuice, vanilla bean and its scraped seeds, orange zest and juice in a saucepan and bring to the boil. Working in batches if necessary, add the persimmon and simmer over low heat for 15 minutes or until just softened (firmer fruit could take up to 25 minutes). Remove the persimmon with a slotted spoon and transfer to a bowl, then simmer the syrup until reduced by half. (The syrup thickens and becomes viscous on cooling, so it may need to be gently reheated before using.)

Preheat a fan-forced oven to 200°C (220°C).

Place the almonds on a baking tray and roast for 6–8 minutes or until golden, checking them frequently to make sure they don't burn. Remove and set aside to cool, then transfer to a food processor and process until finely ground.

Reduce the oven temperature to 170°C fan-forced (190°C). Grease and line the base of a 20 cm springform cake tin with baking paper.

Using an electric mixer, beat the butter with 120 g of the sugar until pale and creamy. Add the yolks one at a time, beating well after adding each one. Stir in the vanilla and ground almonds.

Using a very clean and dry electric mixer, whisk the egg whites with a pinch of salt until soft peaks form. With the motor running, gradually add the remaining sugar, beating well until the mixture is a little glossy and stiff peaks form. Fold a little of the beaten white into the butter and almond mixture and then gently fold in the buckwheat flour. Gently fold in the remainder of the egg whites, taking care not to over-mix and knock too much air out of the beaten egg white. Carefully spoon the batter into the prepared cake tin, then bake the cake for 35–40 minutes; it is ready when a skewer inserted in the centre comes out clean.

Insert a skewer about 20 times into the warm cake, then pour over three-quarters of the reserved persimmon syrup. Leave the cake to cool completely, then remove from the tin. Place a single layer of poached persimmon over the top of the cake, then top with the remaining syrup and spoon the strips of zest on top. Dust with icing sugar, if using, and serve with a jug of double cream and the remaining poached persimmon to the side.

Nat Paull's Braised Sangiovese Peaches with Raspberries

Nat Paull was my apprentice in the last years of the Pheasant Farm restaurant; a more passionate cook would be hard to find. She has a great feel for desserts, and has opened her own cafe in Melbourne, called Beatrix, to showcase her delicious wares. She's always loved braising stone fruits in the oven as it gives a more intense flavour than poaching. Earlier this year, she teamed her braised peaches with some of my vanilla and elderflower ice cream and some gently bruised raspberries, and named it Peach Maggie! Having savoured every mouthful of her wonderful dish, I'm truly honoured. If you can't get perfectly ripe peaches for this, you may need to cook them for slightly longer.

SERVES 8

¾ cup (165 g) caster sugar
1½ cups (375 ml) Sangiovese verjuice
zest from ½ lemon, removed in thin strips with a vegetable peeler, leaving the bitter pith
½ vanilla bean, split and rubbed with some of the sugar
8 ripe white peaches, halved and stones removed
1 punnet fresh raspberries
good-quality vanilla bean ice cream or vanilla and elderflower ice cream, to serve

Preheat a fan-forced oven to 180°C (200°C).

Place the sugar, verjuice, lemon zest and vanilla in a baking dish. Stir to dissolve the sugar. Add the peach halves and gently toss to coat in the verjuice mixture.

Braise the peaches in the oven for 20–30 minutes, spooning the verjuice mixture over the top every 10 minutes, until the peaches are tender and cooked through when pierced with a skewer but not collapsing.

Remove from the oven and loosely cover with foil to create a little steam. Set aside until cool enough to handle, then slip the skins off.

Place the raspberries in a bowl and spoon over ¼ cup (60 ml) of the verjuice syrup. Gently crush the raspberries with the back of a fork.

Divide the peaches among shallow serving bowls. Spoon a little of the verjuice syrup over and scatter with the crushed raspberries. Serve with ice cream.

Quandong Clafoutis

Quandong is our native peach and, whilst well known in South Australia, it deserves wider recognition for its wonderfully intense flavour when dried. There is huge variation in the quality of dried quandongs, so it's worth seeking out ones that are brightly coloured and plump. I reconstitute them in verjuice (as I do all dried fruit), but with quandongs this is also an attempt to counter the high amounts of sugar in which they're so often cooked, so much so that the true flavour of the quandong can be disguised. The trick with clafoutis is to have all your guests at the table and ready so it can be served without delay, as it tends to sink a little as it cools.

SERVES 4–6

---

40 g best-quality dried quandongs
1¼ cups (310 ml) verjuice
⅓ cup (45 g) macadamia nuts
185 g white sugar
50 ml medium-dry sherry
unsalted butter, softened, for greasing
3 lemon myrtle leaves or lemon verbena leaves
1 cup (250 ml) milk
½ cup (75 g) plain flour
2 eggs
1 egg yolk
cream (optional), to serve

Soak the quandongs in verjuice overnight, making sure they are completely covered. Alternatively, place the quandongs and verjuice in a microwave-safe container and microwave on low for 2 minutes, then set aside for 20 minutes to reconstitute. Drain the quandongs (you should end up with about 120 g), reserving the soaking liquid.

Preheat a fan-forced oven to 180°C (200°C).

Place the macadamias on a baking tray and roast for 5–6 minutes, just long enough to refresh them. Set aside to cool, then roughly chop. Leave the oven on, ready for the clafoutis.

Measure ⅔ cup (160 ml) of the reserved soaking liquid and pour into a small saucepan. Add 1 cup (250 ml) water, ½ cup (110 g) of the sugar and the sherry and bring to a simmer over medium heat, stirring to dissolve the sugar. Simmer for 5 minutes, then add the quandongs and simmer for a further 5 minutes or until they're tender but still intact. Remove from the heat and drain the quandongs, reserving the cooking liquid.

Bring the reserved cooking liquid to a boil in a medium-sized saucepan over high heat, then simmer for 15 minutes or until reduced to a thin syrup; you should have about ½ cup (125 ml). Set aside.

Lightly grease a 1 litre baking dish with butter. Spread the quandongs over the base of the dish.

Place the lemon myrtle leaves or lemon verbena leaves and milk in a small saucepan and bring just to a simmer over medium heat, then immediately turn the heat off and leave to infuse for 10 minutes. Strain the milk, discarding the leaves.

Sift the flour and remaining ⅓ cup (75 g) sugar into a mixing bowl, then make a well in the centre. Add the eggs and yolk and using a whisk, gradually whisk the flour and eggs to combine. Pour in the warm milk and continue whisking to form a smooth batter.

Pour the batter over the quandongs, sprinkle with the macadamias and bake for 20–25 minutes or until just set, golden and puffed.

Serve the clafoutis immediately. Pour over some reserved syrup and accompany with cream, if desired.

Sangiovese Verjuice and Sparkling Pinot Noir Jelly with Nectarines

Sparkling, wobbly jellies filled with fruit are so beautiful that sometimes I make them in glass dishes to show them off in all their glory, in case I lose my nerve when it comes to turning them out. This jelly would be equally good with fresh nectarines or any other soft fruit, first poached then the skins slipped off to show the beautiful colours of the fruit (think of the jelly as a foundation on which you can build the flavours). To serve, this needs nothing other than runny cream.

SERVES 8

½ cup (100 g) dried nectarines
½ cup (125 ml) Sangiovese verjuice, plus about 1 cup (250 ml) extra
1 × 750 ml bottle sparkling Pinot Noir
¼ cup (55 g) caster sugar
9 × 2 g gold-strength gelatine leaves
pure cream, to serve

Place the nectarines and the ½ cup (125 ml) of verjuice in a bowl and leave overnight to reconstitute. Alternatively, place the nectarines and verjuice in a microwave-safe container and microwave on low for 2 minutes, then set aside for 20 minutes to reconstitute. (Most of the verjuice will be absorbed.) Drain the nectarines in a fine-meshed sieve placed over a measuring jug, then add enough of the extra verjuice to bring the total quantity up to 1 cup (250 ml).

Place the sparkling wine in a stainless-steel saucepan, then bring to the boil over high heat. Remove from the heat, then add the verjuice and sugar and stir to dissolve the sugar. Set aside.

Soak the gelatine leaves in a bowl of cold water for 5 minutes or until softened. Squeeze out any excess liquid and stir the gelatine into the warm wine mixture until dissolved. Set aside to cool to room temperature (this could take up to 30 minutes, depending on the weather, but check the mixture every now and then to make sure it doesn't set).

Pour a 1 cm thick layer of the wine mixture into a 1 litre jelly mould, then refrigerate for 10 minutes to set slightly (it should feel a little set when touched with a fingertip). Arrange one-third of the nectarines, cut-side up, over the jelly layer, then pour in enough of the jelly mixture to cover the nectarines. Return the mould to the fridge and leave for 30–45 minutes or until slightly set. Repeat this layering process twice more with the remaining two-thirds of the nectarines and jelly mixture, refrigerating for 30–45 minutes after adding each layer to allow the jelly to set slightly before adding the next layer. When finished, cover with plastic film and refrigerate overnight.

To turn the jelly out, dip the base of the mould into a bowl of hot water for 30 seconds, then carefully invert the jelly onto a serving plate; if the jelly does not fall out easily, leave the mould inverted on the plate and wet a tea towel with hot water, then wring it out and place the tea towel over the mould to help loosen the jelly.

Serve the jelly with cream alongside.

Dianne's Scones with Mulberry and Verjuice Jam

Dianne Wooldridge is our master sconemaker at the Farmshop. In four years of filming *The Cook and the Chef*, she helped a great deal in many ways, but I think it was the morning-tea scones she whipped up without a second thought that endeared her most to the crew. I have to say she doesn't even weigh anything, but just throws the ingredients together, so we had to watch her very carefully to get this recipe right. Chris Wotton, my product development chef, picked the mulberries to make the jam. Our mulberry tree is of the old-fashioned variety that makes your hands purple as you pick the berries, but who cares when the flavour of the darkest, ripest ones are so special that it's hard not to just keep on eating as you're picking? This makes a small amount of jam and it's very quick to make: great for when guests pop around at short notice. It doesn't set firm like regular jam, but rather is a nice syrupy consistency – perfect for dolloping onto scones.

MAKES 24

4 cups (600 g) plain flour, plus extra for dusting
1½ tablespoons baking powder
pinch of salt
⅓ cup (55 g) icing sugar
2 cups (500 ml) thickened cream
⅔ cup (160 ml) milk
whipped cream, to serve

MULBERRY AND VERJUICE JAM
300 g mulberries
100 ml verjuice
125 g caster sugar
1 tablespoon lemon juice

To make the jam, place the mulberries, verjuice and caster sugar in a saucepan over high heat, then bring to the boil and boil rapidly for 5 minutes. Add the lemon juice and boil for a further 5 minutes or until the jam is a syrupy consistency. Leave to cool for 15 minutes, then pour into a warm jar and seal.

Preheat a fan-forced oven to 180°C (200°C) and line a baking tray with baking paper.

Sift together the flour, baking powder, salt and icing sugar into a large bowl. Make a well in the centre and gradually fold in the cream and the milk until you have a soft dough (it shouldn't be sloppy or dry – you may need to use more or less cream and milk, depending on the moisture content of the flour). Take care not to over-mix.

Turn out the dough onto a lightly floured bench and gently pat down to flatten it out to a thickness of 3 cm. Use a 5 cm round cutter to cut out 24 discs and place them close together on the prepared baking tray. Bake for 20–25 minutes or until golden and well risen.

Serve the scones with a bowl of mulberry and verjuice jam and some whipped cream to the side.

Burnt Fig Jam and Verjuice Semi Freddo with Almond Praline

By now, I think it's pretty well known how much I love burnt fig jam. It came about from one of those happy accidents in life: when my mother cooked her fig jam, she always managed to burn it, and I always loved that this stopped the jam from being super sweet. The burn is essential for me in my commercially-made fig jam, and believe me, it takes great skill to replicate in large quantities! I have to admit my fig growers in the Riverland (generally wholehearted supporters of mine) think I'm barking up the wrong tree with this one – they don't quite know how to tell me they really don't like it. Conversely, I'm reluctant to confess that I find their beautifully-made fig jam much too sweet.

SERVES 8–10

---

120 ml verjuice
6 egg yolks
150 g caster sugar
1 sprig rosemary
100 ml full-cream milk
2 cups (500 ml) thickened cream
finely grated zest of 1 lemon
1 × 300 g jar Maggie Beer Burnt Fig Jam

ALMOND PRALINE
1 cup (80 g) flaked almonds
350 g caster sugar

Simmer the verjuice in a small saucepan over medium heat for 5 minutes or until reduced by half. Set aside.

Using an electric mixer with a whisk attachment, whisk the egg yolks and sugar for 4 minutes or until thick and pale.

Gently bruise the rosemary sprig with a mortar and pestle to release the oils.

Combine the milk, 150 ml of the cream, the lemon zest and rosemary sprig in a saucepan over medium heat and stir continuously until the mixture is very hot; do not let it boil. With the electric mixer on low, immediately strain the milk mixture through a fine-meshed sieve into the egg mixture, whisking it slowly to incorporate. Add the reduced verjuice and whisk until incorporated, then cover with plastic film and refrigerate until cooled completely.

Using hand-held electric beaters, whisk the remaining cream until medium peaks form. Fold one-quarter of the whipped cream at a time into the cooled egg mixture.

Line a 1 litre loaf tin with baking paper, leaving 5 cm hanging over the edge of the tin. Pour one-third of the custard into the tin, then cover with the overhanging baking paper and plastic film and freeze for 1½–2 hours or until just set.

Remove the semi freddo from the freezer, then spoon over half the burnt fig jam and top with another one-third of the custard mixture. Cover and return to the freezer for 1½ hours, then top with the remaining jam followed by the remaining custard. Leave to set overnight in the freezer.

Meanwhile, to make the almond praline, preheat a fan-forced oven to 200°C (220°C).

Place the almonds on a baking tray and roast for 5–8 minutes or until golden, checking them frequently to make sure they don't burn. Remove from the oven and transfer to a clean baking tray lined with baking paper, then set aside to cool.

Place the sugar and ⅔ cup (160 ml) water in a heavy-based saucepan over high heat and stir gently to dissolve the sugar. Bring to the boil and stop stirring, then immediately reduce the heat to low and cook for 12–15 minutes or until the caramel is a light-golden colour. Remove the pan from the heat immediately and set aside to cool for 2 minutes, watching the caramel closely at this stage as it will continue to cook and go slighter darker as it cools.

Pour the caramel evenly over the almonds to form a 2 mm thick layer. Set the praline aside for 30 minutes or until cooled completely, then break into shards.

Take the overhanging baking paper and gently lift the semi freddo out of the tin, then place on a chopping board. Use a hot sharp knife to cut it into 1.5 cm thick slices, then serve with shards of almond praline.

Maggie's Constitution Cake

During my tenure as Senior Australian of the Year, I was so proud to be asked to make our nation's first ever Constitution Cake. I presented the cake on Constitution Eve at the High Court in Canberra, and spoke of the thinking behind the making of the cake. I wanted to bring together the beautiful flavours of our native fruits (the Davidson's plums, quandongs and muntries) that marry so well with the dried fruit and almonds of the early settlers, and the crowning glory of the macadamia paste. Muntries are not easy to find; you'll have to seek them out from specialist native food suppliers, and they're usually supplied frozen. This cake is so beautifully rich in every sense of the word that just a small slice is needed. Try one with a glass of Tokay, and celebrate a part of our heritage.

SERVES 16–20

1½ cups (375 ml) verjuice
50 g caster sugar
120 g dried quandongs
120 g dried currants
120 g macadamia nuts
60 g blanched almonds
100 g icing sugar, sifted
1 egg yolk
120 g dark brown sugar
180 g unsalted butter, chopped
4 eggs
180 g self-raising flour
½ teaspoon ground cinnamon
½ teaspoon ground nutmeg
180 g Davidson's plums, sliced and stones removed
120 g muntries
120 g candied mixed peel
finely grated zest of 1 lemon

Combine the verjuice and sugar in a saucepan and add the quandongs. Set aside for 30 minutes to reconstitute. Transfer to the stove, bring to the boil and cook for 5 minutes over high heat. Remove from the heat, add the currants and leave to soak for 1 hour to soften, then drain, reserving the syrup, and set aside.

Preheat a fan-forced oven to 220°C (240°C) and grease and line a 20 cm springform cake tin with baking paper.

Place the macadamias and almonds on separate baking trays and roast for 6–8 minutes or until golden, checking them frequently to make sure they don't burn. Remove and set aside to cool. Reduce the oven temperature to 170°C fan-forced (190°C).

Process the macadamias in a food processor until finely ground, then add the icing sugar and egg yolk and pulse to form a stiff paste. Set aside.

Using an electric mixer, cream the brown sugar with the butter until fluffy. Beat in the eggs one at a time, adding a spoonful of the flour if the mixture curdles.

With a metal spoon, fold in the rest of the flour, together with the spices, plums, muntries, mixed peel, lemon zest, almonds and currants and quandongs and their reserved syrup, to form a soft batter.

Spoon half the batter into the prepared tin, then spread the macadamia paste over the batter and top with the remaining batter. Bake for 2½ hours or until a skewer inserted in the centre of the cake comes out clean (check after 1½ hours: if the top is browning too quickly, cover the cake with foil for the last hour of cooking).

Leave the cake to cool a little in the tin before turning it out to cool on a wire rack.

Serve cut into small slices. Store the leftovers in an airtight container.

Grilled Figs with Almond Crisp and Verjuice Sabayon

This year we had the best fig harvest ever. Not only did we get a very large crop, but the fact that the season was so late meant that the birds weren't the perennial pest they normally are. Every two days I picked bowls and bowls of figs, so we enjoyed figs in every way imaginable. Figs are such a fragile fruit; I often think that you can only truly appreciate how wonderful they are when you have your own fig tree. It takes time to know exactly when to pick, as there is a subtle colour change just before the figs are at their peak. Leave it too late and you'll have figs that have gone too far and are only worth cooking for jam. This recipe calls for ripe figs: if your figs are on the firm side, they may need to be cooked for a little longer.

SERVES 6

1½ tablespoons vino cotto
1 tablespoon extra virgin olive oil
12 ripe figs

ALMOND CRISP
50 ml verjuice
⅓ cup (75 g) soft brown sugar
1 cup (125 g) flaked almonds

VERJUICE SABAYON
1½ cups (375 ml) Sangiovese verjuice
3 egg yolks
50 g caster sugar

Preheat a fan-forced oven to 180°C (200°C).

To make the almond crisp, place the verjuice, brown sugar and almonds in a bowl and toss to combine well. Spread the almond mixture evenly on a baking tray lined with baking paper. Bake for 9 minutes, then rotate the tray and cook for another 9 minutes or until the almonds are pale golden, watching carefully in case the sugar burns. Set aside to cool, then break into shards.

To make the verjuice sabayon, simmer the verjuice in a saucepan over medium heat for 10 minutes or until reduced to 150 ml. Set aside to cool to room temperature.

Bring a saucepan one-third filled with water to a simmer over a medium heat, then reduce the heat to low. Place the egg yolks and sugar in a heatproof bowl that fits snugly over the saucepan, taking care that the bottom of the bowl does not touch the simmering water. Slowly add the cooled verjuice a little at a time, whisking the mixture constantly for 8 minutes, or until it thickens, forms ribbons and holds its shape when lifted with a spoon. Remove the sabayon from the heat and cover the surface closely with plastic film.

Preheat a barbecue grill plate or chargrill pan to high.

Combine the vino cotto and olive oil in a small bowl. Cut the figs in half lengthways, then brush the cut surface with the vino cotto mixture. Place cut-side down on the very hot barbecue or chargrill pan and cook for 2–3 minutes or until well caramelised.

Serve the figs with the almond crisp and warm sabayon to the side.

Grilled Apricots with Quick Apricot Ice Cream and Dutch Ginger Cake

Recently we stayed with my husband Colin's cousin, Howard, and his wife, Dot, at Jurien Bay in Western Australia and were spoilt with local lobster cooked every imaginable way. We also enjoyed that old country custom of afternoon tea, which I fear has been all but forgotten in this fast-paced life we live. Dot made this delicious ginger cake, which is actually more like a shortbread biscuit, and I just had to ask for the recipe. Whether served simply with a cup of coffee or tea or as a crunchy contrast to this very quick ice cream, I think you'll love it too.

SERVES 4

⅓ cup (120 g) honey
½ cup (125 ml) verjuice
2 teaspoons finely sliced glace ginger
1 tablespoon rosemary leaves
6 large ripe apricots, cut in half and stones removed

DUTCH GINGER CAKE

185 g unsalted butter, chopped
1¾ cups (260 g) plain flour
table salt
⅔ cup (150 g) caster sugar
140 g glace ginger, roughly chopped
1 egg, beaten
60 g blanched almonds

QUICK APRICOT ICE CREAM

350 g ripe apricots, cut in half and stones removed
2 tablespoons honey
130 g creme fraiche
50 ml verjuice
½ teaspoon finely chopped rosemary leaves

To make the ice cream, place the apricot halves in the freezer for 30 minutes or until slightly firm, then immediately transfer them to a food processor and blend for 20 seconds or until they resemble coarse breadcrumbs. Add the remaining ingredients and blend for a further 40 seconds or until smooth. If not serving straightaway or if you'd like a firmer set, transfer the mixture to a chilled bowl and pop into the freezer to firm up. Remove from the freezer a few minutes before serving.

To make the Dutch ginger cake, preheat a fan-forced oven to 180°C (200°C). Lightly grease a 22 cm springform cake tin and line the base with baking paper.

Melt the butter in a small saucepan over low heat, then set aside to cool for 5 minutes.

Meanwhile, sift the flour and ¼ teaspoon salt into a large mixing bowl and stir in the sugar and chopped ginger. Tip in most of the beaten egg (reserving about 1 teaspoon for the glaze) and the melted butter and mix well with your hands until an oily dough forms.

Press the mixture evenly into the prepared tin and brush over the remaining beaten egg. Arrange the almonds evenly on top, and bake for 30–35 minutes or until the cake is golden and firm to the touch. Remove from the oven and leave to cool in the tin.

Place the honey, verjuice, sliced ginger and rosemary in a saucepan and bring to the boil over high heat. Reduce the heat to low and simmer for 2 minutes to allow the flavours to infuse the syrup, then strain.

Preheat the grill to high and line the grill tray with foil. Arrange the apricot halves cut-side up on the tray, and brush about half the syrup over the top.

Positioning the grill tray so that the apricots are about 6 cm from the heat, grill for 6–8 minutes, watching carefully, until the cut-side is dark golden and caramelised and the fruit is slightly softened.

Serve three apricot halves per person with a dollop of apricot ice cream and a thin wedge of Dutch ginger cake. Drizzle the remaining syrup over the fruit.

Verjuice, Poached Apple and Olive Oil Upside Down Puddings

I tend to call these puddings rather than cakes because they are incredibly moist and pudding-like if eaten straight from the oven. As they cool though, they cook that little bit more in their residual heat, so then you might just as easily call them cakes. Either way, they are delicious. I like to use Pink Lady apples for their amazing flavour and their delicate colour that shines through when cooked. (I used to think only of Granny Smiths when choosing cooking apples, as they really suit my not-so-sweet palate, so the Pink Ladies were a bit of a revelation to me.) These puddings will fall as you take them out of the oven, so don't be too alarmed. You could also make one large pudding in a 20 cm springform cake tin; just bake it for 35–40 minutes or until the pudding springs back to the touch.

MAKES 6

---

unsalted butter, for greasing
3 eggs, separated
125 g caster sugar
½ cup (75 g) plain flour
½ teaspoon baking powder
¼ cup (60 ml) extra virgin olive oil

POACHED APPLE
4 large Pink Lady apples, peeled, cored and each cut into eight wedges
300 ml verjuice
1 sprig rosemary, leaves picked and finely chopped
1 tablespoon extra virgin olive oil
¼ cup (55 g) caster sugar

Preheat a fan-forced oven to 180°C (200°C) and grease six 250 ml ramekins with butter.

For the poached apple, place the apple, verjuice and rosemary in a deep frying pan, cover with a lid and bring to the boil over high heat. Reduce the heat to medium and simmer for 8–10 minutes or until the apple is just tender. Remove the apple with a slotted spoon, transfer to a plate and set aside. Remove ¼ cup (60 ml) of the poaching liquid and reserve for the pudding batter. Transfer the remaining poaching liquid to a small saucepan and set aside.

Wipe the frying pan out with paper towel, pour in the olive oil and return to the stove on medium–high heat. Add the apple and cook for 2–3 minutes on each side or until just starting to turn golden brown. Divide the apple among the bases of the ramekins and set aside.

Add the sugar to the saucepan of poaching liquid and bring to the boil over medium heat, stirring to dissolve the sugar. Simmer for 5 minutes or until the liquid has reduced to 100 ml. Set aside to use as a glaze to brush over the puddings.

Using an electric mixer, whisk the egg whites until soft peaks form. With the motor running, gradually add half of the sugar, continuing to whisk until the sugar has dissolved and the whites have become glossy and form firm peaks.

In a separate bowl, beat the yolks and remaining sugar with hand-held electric beaters until pale. Sift in the flour and baking powder and stir to combine. Pour in the oil and the reserved ¼ cup (60 ml) poaching liquid and mix to combine. Gently fold in one-third of the egg white until combined, then fold in another third to combine, and finally fold in the remaining third.

Spoon the batter into the prepared ramekins. Bake the puddings for 15–20 minutes or until well risen and golden brown; a skewer inserted in the centre should come out clean.

Leave to cool for a few minutes and then invert the puddings onto serving plates. Brush with the verjuice glaze, then drizzle over any remaining glaze. Serve warm or at room temperature.

Saffron-roasted Pears with Verjuice Panna Cotta

Adding saffron to a sugar syrup gives it the most beautiful colour and an amazing depth of flavour, with just an edge of bitterness. The pears are simmered in the syrup before being roasted, when they take on a distinctive rich burnish (depending on the ripeness of the pears and your oven, this can take up to 40 minutes). The panna cotta is a great foil for this richness, and is best if made the day before. (Or, if you're not in the mood, just serve the pears with a very generous blob of thick cream – it will still go down beautifully!)

SERVES 6

½ cup (110 g) caster sugar
2 cups (500 ml) verjuice
1 cup (250 ml) medium-dry sherry (optional, can be replaced by ½ cup [125 ml] each verjuice and water)
12 saffron threads
6 small pears, peeled, plus 1 pear, peeled, cored and chopped

VERJUICE PANNA COTTA
360 ml verjuice
400 ml pure cream
½ cup (125 ml) milk
¼ cup (55 g) caster sugar
2 × 2 g gold-strength gelatine leaves

To make the verjuice panna cotta, place the verjuice in a small saucepan and bring to the boil over high heat. Simmer for 12–14 minutes or until reduced to 100 ml. Set aside to cool. Place the cream, milk and sugar in a small saucepan and bring just to the boil, then remove from the heat immediately.

Soften the gelatine in a bowl of cold water for 5 minutes and squeeze dry. Add the gelatine to the hot cream mixture and stir well, then set aside to cool for 10 minutes (it should register 50°C on a sugar thermometer). Add the reduced verjuice, stirring to mix well. Divide the mixture among six 100 ml moulds. Transfer to a baking tray, cover well with plastic film and refrigerate for at least 4 hours or until set (overnight is best, if you have time).

Place the sugar, verjuice, sherry, saffron and 2 cups (500 ml) water in a wide-based saucepan large enough to accommodate the pears, then bring to the boil over high heat. Reduce the heat, add the chopped pear, cover with a tight-fitting lid and simmer for 20 minutes. Gently slip the whole pears into the syrup, then cover with a round of baking paper and the lid and simmer for 20 minutes or until tender when pierced with a skewer.

Leave the pears to cool for 10 minutes in the syrup, then carefully transfer to a plate. Strain the syrup through a fine-meshed sieve into a saucepan, discarding the solids, then bring the syrup to the boil over high heat and simmer until it has reduced by half. Transfer 1 cup (250 ml) syrup to a small saucepan (reserving the remaining syrup for serving), then simmer over medium heat for 10 minutes or until reduced to a thick honey-like consistency.

Preheat a fan-forced oven to 220°C (240°C).

When the pears are cool enough to handle, cut them in half lengthways. Place the pears cut-side up on a baking tray. Using a pastry brush, coat each pear with a little of the reduced syrup, then roast, brushing the pears with the reduced syrup every 10 minutes, for 15–25 minutes or until they are a wonderfully deep-golden colour, taking care that they don't burn.

To turn out the panna cotta, use your fingertip to gently press around the edge to break the seal. Quickly invert each mould onto a serving plate and the panna cotta should drop out. Divide the saffron-roasted pears among the plates, spoon over some of the reserved syrup, then serve.

Verjuice Custards with Bergamot-braised Raisin Clusters

As recipes often do, this one has had various incarnations over the years. The latest was when I joined two of my great friends and former colleagues, Steve Flamsteed and Nat Paull, for a 'Memories of the Pheasant Farm' masterclass at the Melbourne Food and Wine Festival in 2009. Nat took these sublime custards to another dimension by serving them with braised raisin clusters. As the custards are so delicate, it's worth making them the day before and refrigerating them overnight to make them easier to handle. A word of caution: the custard will curdle if overcooked, so keep a close eye on it and treat the cooking time and temperature given here as a guide only, as every oven is so different. The bergamot-braised raisins can be made in advance and stored in an airtight container in the fridge for several weeks.

SERVES 6

350 ml cream (40–45% fat)
1 sprig rosemary or bay leaf, crushed
1½ cups (375 ml) verjuice
2 × 55 g eggs
5–6 egg yolks (you need 100 g egg yolk)
100 g caster sugar

BERGAMOT-BRAISED RAISIN CLUSTERS
250 g muscatel raisins on stems
125 g caster sugar
2 g Earl Grey tea leaves

Line a roasting pan (mine is 20 cm × 25 cm × 3 cm deep) with a Chux (J-cloth), then place in six 125 ml dariole moulds. Place the cream and rosemary sprig or bay leaf in a small saucepan over medium heat and bring to simmering point. Remove from the heat and leave to infuse for 10 minutes. Bring the verjuice to a simmer in a small saucepan over medium heat and cook for 7 minutes or until reduced by almost half; do not let it boil. Set aside and keep warm.

Remove and discard the rosemary or bay leaf from the cream. Place the cream over medium heat and bring to simmering point.

Preheat a fan-forced oven to 120°C (140°C).

Place the eggs, egg yolks and caster sugar in a bowl and whisk gently to just combine; take care not to incorporate too much air. Whisking continuously, add the warm verjuice in a slow, steady, thin stream until incorporated. Still whisking continuously, add the hot cream in a slow, steady, thin stream until incorporated.

Gently pour the mixture evenly into the moulds through a small fine-meshed sieve to eliminate any air bubbles. Carefully pour boiling water into the pan until it reaches two-thirds of the way up the sides of the moulds.

Taking care, transfer the roasting pan to the oven and bake the custards for 1 hour or until soft-set. To test, press the surface lightly with a fingertip; the custard should feel set but not firm. Remove the roasting pan from the oven and leave the custards to cool in the water bath. Remove the moulds from the water bath, then cover with plastic film and refrigerate overnight.

For the raisin clusters, place the raisins in a bowl and cover with boiling water. Set aside to plump for 45 minutes.

Place the sugar and 1½ cups (375 ml) water in a small saucepan over medium heat and bring to a simmer, stirring to dissolve the sugar. Simmer until reduced to ½ cup (125 ml), then set aside.

Meanwhile, place the tea in a small heatproof bowl or jug and pour over ¼ cup (60 ml) boiling water, then leave to infuse for 5 minutes. Strain through a fine-meshed sieve into the pan of sugar syrup.

Drain the raisins and add to the pan, then place over medium heat and cook for 1 minute, stirring gently to coat the raisins in syrup. Remove from the heat and cool to room temperature, then divide into 12 clusters.

To turn out the custards, use your fingertip to gently press around the edge to break the seal. Invert each mould over a small plate, then squeeze a little so the custard releases and drops gently onto the plate. Place a raisin cluster to the side, spoon over a little syrup and serve.

Verjuice-pickled Prunes with Blue Cheese Paste and Walnuts

Prunes certainly divide people, but I come out on the side of loving them, and always have. Over the years, I've poached them in tea, in sherry, or in a combination of both, but I've now decided this is my favourite poaching liquid for prunes to serve with cheese. I have used Picon, a blue cheese, here, but any other Spanish blue cheese or a gorgonzola piccante will do; the bluer the cheese, the better, I think. Serve this as a cheese course at the end of a meal with a glass of Seppeltsfield Amontillado sherry, or with drinks by the fire in winter, with a warming glass of Muscat.

SERVES 6–8

- 1 cup (250 ml) boiling water
- 2 teaspoons orange pekoe tea leaves
- 1 sprig rosemary
- 1 cinnamon stick
- 8 black peppercorns
- zest and juice of 1 orange, zest removed in thin strips with a vegetable peeler, leaving the bitter pith
- ¾ cup (180 ml) Sangiovese verjuice
- ¼ cup (55 g) sugar
- 250 g pitted prunes
- 30 g walnuts
- 1 loaf walnut bread
- 60 g unsalted butter, melted
- 120 g blue cheese
- 120 g mascarpone

Pour the boiling water over the tea leaves in a heatproof jug or bowl and leave to infuse for 3 minutes, then strain through a fine-meshed sieve into a small saucepan. Add the rosemary, cinnamon, peppercorns, orange zest and juice, verjuice and sugar. Bring the mixture to the boil over high heat, then boil rapidly for 5 minutes or until the liquid has reduced to ½ cup (125 ml). Reduce the heat to medium, then add the prunes and simmer for 4 minutes. Remove from the heat and set aside to cool.

Preheat a fan-forced oven to 200°C (220°C).

Place the walnuts on a baking tray and roast for 5 minutes or until golden, checking them frequently to make sure they don't burn. Immediately wrap in a clean tea towel and rub to remove the skins. Shake the walnuts in a sieve to get rid of the skins, then set aside to cool.

Cut the walnut bread into 8 mm thick slices and brush one side of each slice with melted butter. Place the bread on a baking tray, buttered-side up, and toast in the oven for 6–8 minutes or until golden.

Place the blue cheese in a bowl and mash with the back of a fork to soften, then fold in the mascarpone. Transfer the prune mixture to a serving dish, then serve with the toasted bread, the blue cheese paste and the walnuts alongside.

Chris Wotton's Meringue Roulade with Verjuice Creme Curd and Cherries

Chris is the only chef we employ in the business and he works with me every day on product development. It's made my life so much easier. With so many ideas in this head of mine, and so little time just to be in the kitchen and trial them, Chris undertakes this role with enthusiasm. He cooks, we taste, he cooks again. Sometimes an idea will take two months to get right, or even two years! Chris's energy and willingness to adapt to my unstructured way of thinking and cooking has meant that every day is full of optimism. Chris loves desserts, while I love savoury dishes, so we continually learn from each other.

SERVES 8

olive oil spray, for greasing
4 egg whites
table salt
180 g caster sugar
1 tablespoon verjuice
1 teaspoon cornflour

VERJUICE CURD
120 g unsalted butter, softened
100 g caster sugar
3 × 50 g eggs
4 egg yolks (from 50 g eggs)
½ cup (125 ml) verjuice
finely grated zest of 1 lemon

VERJUICE CREME
⅓ cup (80 ml) verjuice
½ × 2 g gold-strength gelatine leaf
½ cup (125 ml) thickened cream

VERJUICE CHERRIES
1½ cups (375 ml) verjuice
2 tablespoons caster sugar, or to taste
450 g cherries

To make the verjuice curd, place all the ingredients in a saucepan over low–medium heat, whisking continuously until the butter has melted and the ingredients are well combined. Using a wooden spoon, stir constantly for 15 minutes or until the curd thickens and coats the back of the spoon; the temperature should register 84°C on a digital thermometer. (Don't try to cook this more quickly over a higher heat or the egg will scramble.) Remove from the heat, transfer to a clean bowl and cover the surface closely with plastic film. Cool in the fridge.

To make the verjuice creme, place the verjuice in a small saucepan over high heat, bring to the boil and reduce to 1½ tablespoons, then remove from the heat. Soften the gelatine in a bowl of cold water for 5 minutes, then squeeze out the excess water. Add the gelatine to the warm verjuice and stir until it has dissolved. Set aside until the mixture is lukewarm. Whisk the cream in the bowl of an electric mixer until firm peaks form, then add the chilled verjuice curd and cooled verjuice and gelatine mixture and continue to whisk on high speed for 1 minute. Cover with plastic film and refrigerate until required.

PICTURED OVERLEAF >

Preheat a fan-forced oven to 170°C (190°C).

Spray a 30 cm × 20 cm × 3 cm baking tin with olive oil spray and line with baking paper, then spray the baking paper with the oil spray (this helps to ensure that the paper does not stick when you try to remove the meringue after baking). Using an electric mixer set on medium–high speed, whisk the egg whites and a pinch of salt until soft peaks form. Add the caster sugar, a little at a time, whisking well after each addition. Continue to whisk for 4 minutes. Turn the mixer down to low–medium, then add the verjuice and cornflour and whisk for 1 minute or until well combined. Spread the meringue mixture into the prepared tin, leaving a 1 cm border around the edge. Using the tines of a fork, make grooves along the length of the meringue.

Bake the meringue on the middle shelf of the oven for 16 minutes or until it has a slight crust on top (if your oven bakes unevenly, you may need to rotate the tray after 8 minutes). Remove the baking tin from the oven, then slide the meringue onto a cooling rack and leave it to cool for 5 minutes.

Line a baking tray with baking paper and place gently, baking paper-side down, on top of the meringue. Holding both the cooling rack and baking tray, flip the meringue over and remove the top layer of baking paper. Leave the meringue to cool completely.

Spread the verjuice creme curd evenly over the meringue using a palette knife. Gently roll up the meringue, starting from one of the long sides, enclosing the verjuice creme curd. Secure the roulade with the baking paper, then carefully transfer to a baking tray and refrigerate for at least 1 hour to set.

Meanwhile, for the verjuice cherries, place the verjuice and sugar in a small saucepan over high heat and reduce to ½ cup (125 ml). Reduce the heat to low–medium, then add the cherries and cook for 5 minutes or until the verjuice syrup has reduced to about 1½ tablespoons, tossing the pan gently every few minutes to stop the cherries from catching on the base. Transfer to a bowl and serve warm or at room temperature.

Remove the baking paper from the roulade. If you have a kitchen blowtorch, lightly toast the surface of the roulade. Cut into slices and serve with verjuice cherries.

Chocolate, Quince and Almond Tart

I love the idea of setting fruit in a tart filling. Here, the poached quince cuts through the richness of the chocolate and gives the tart a luscious deep ruby-red colour when cut.

SERVES 12

750 g quinces, peeled, cored and cut into large wedges, cores and skin reserved
squeeze of lemon juice
200 ml verjuice, plus 100 ml extra
¾ cup (165 g) caster sugar
1 quantity Sour-cream Pastry (see page 193)
dark Dutch-process cocoa powder, to serve
whipped cream, to serve

CHOCOLATE ALMOND CREAM
120 g unsalted butter, softened
150 g caster sugar
2 eggs
1 egg yolk
⅓ cup (80 ml) vino cotto
50 g dark Dutch-process cocoa powder
200 g ground almonds

Preheat a fan-forced oven to 170°C (190°C).

Place the quince wedges in a bowl of cold water with a squeeze of lemon to prevent them discolouring. Wrap and tie the quince cores and skin in a piece of muslin, then place in a heavy-based ovenproof saucepan or enamelled cast-iron casserole with the verjuice, sugar and 300 ml water. Bring to the boil over high heat, stirring to dissolve the sugar. Add the drained quince and bring back to the boil, then cover with a tight-fitting lid.

Transfer the casserole to the oven and roast the quince for 1 hour, then gently toss, taking care not to break up the wedges. Return to the oven and cook for another 2 hours or until the quince is tender and deep ruby red but still maintaining its shape, checking every 15–20 minutes to make sure the liquid has not evaporated; add some extra verjuice if necessary to prevent the quince from catching. (The liquid should reduce to a small amount of syrup in the base of the pan.) Remove the quince from the pan and place on a cooling rack or paper-towel-lined plate to drain excess syrup. Set aside to cool.

Increase the oven temperature to 200°C fan-forced (220°C).

To make the chocolate almond cream, place the butter and sugar in an electric mixer, then process for 6 minutes or until light and creamy. Add the eggs and yolk, one at a time and mixing after adding each one, then add the cocoa and vino cotto and mix for a further 1 minute. Add the ground almonds and mix until well combined. Set aside.

Divide the sour-cream pastry in two, with one piece slightly larger than the other. Wrap both pieces in plastic film. Chill the larger piece in the refrigerator for at least 20 minutes and freeze the other piece for another use.

Grease a 24 cm tart tin with a removable base. Roll out the pastry on a lightly floured bench until 2.5 mm thick, then use to line the tart tin. Cut off the excess pastry around the edge, leaving 5 mm to allow for shrinkage as it cooks. Refrigerate for 15 minutes.

Prick the pastry base with a fork, then line with foil, fill with pastry weights and blind bake for 15 minutes. Remove the foil and weights and bake for a further 5 minutes or until the pastry looks dry. Remove from the oven and leave for 10–15 minutes or until cool.

Reduce the oven temperature to 175°C fan-forced (195°C).

Spread one-third of the chocolate almond cream over the base of the tart shell, then top with the quince. Dot the remaining chocolate almond cream over the quince.

Bake the tart for 50 minutes–1 hour or until the chocolate almond cream is cooked in the centre and the surface of the tart is golden (if the surface is browning too quickly, reduce the oven temperature to 165°C fan-forced [185°C] and continue baking until the centre is cooked through).

Remove the tart from the oven and leave to cool completely in the tin. Dust with cocoa powder before slicing and serving with whipped cream.

Apricot Bread and Butter Pudding

Who doesn't love a bread and butter pudding? I know I do – the smell of the slightly burnt edges of the bread straight out of the oven followed by the flavour of the unctuous custard is hard to resist. Here, it's sweetness is tempered by the piquancy of beautiful South Australian apricots. There is such a difference in the quality of our local dried apricots compared to imported ones – I urge you to buy Australian. Not only is this important to prevent our apricot growers being forced to rip out all their trees because they can't compete with the cheap imports (come to think of it, important isn't a strong enough word; it's absolutely essential that we support our local growers), but the flavour is far superior. They are the only ones I'll ever use.

SERVES 6–8

240 g Australian dried apricots
100 ml verjuice
20 g unsalted butter, plus extra for greasing
4–6 slices white bread, crusts removed, rolled between two pieces of baking paper with a rolling pin
550 ml milk
450 ml pure cream
½ vanilla bean
zest from 1 lemon, removed in thin strips with a vegetable peeler, leaving the bitter pith
6 eggs
⅓ cup (75 g) caster sugar

Soak the apricots in the verjuice overnight (or for at least several hours). Alternatively, place the apricots and the verjuice in a microwave-safe container and microwave on low for 2 minutes, then set aside for 20 minutes to reconstitute. Drain off any liquid that remains.

Preheat a fan-forced oven to 140°C (160°C) and grease a 1.5 litre baking dish (about 12 cm × 17 cm and 6 cm deep).

Butter one side of the bread slices, then grill them on both sides until golden.

Place half the drained apricots over the base of the dish, then arrange the slices of bread on top. Transfer the dish to a large roasting pan.

Meanwhile, bring the milk, cream, vanilla and lemon zest to a simmer in a saucepan over medium heat, then remove from the heat and set aside for 10 minutes to allow the flavours to infuse. Remove the lemon zest and vanilla bean with tongs and scrape the vanilla seeds back into the milk mix.

Beat the eggs with the sugar in a large bowl until combined.

Stir the hot milk mixture into the egg mixture until combined, then carefully pour over the bread. Add the remaining apricots, then pour enough boiling water into the roasting pan to come two-thirds of the way up the sides of the dish. Bake for 45–55 minutes or until the custard is just set, then leave to cool for 15 minutes before serving.

Apricot and Almond Tart

This tart speaks of the Barossa and the Riverland. I've used beautiful Australian dried apricots for this – indeed local ones from Blanchetown that are decidedly juicier and plumper than regular dried apricots (you may need to use more apricots in this dish if yours are smaller, but just make sure they're Australian!). The almond filling (called frangipane) is a great favourite of ours at the Farmshop – we make a tart with it every day of the year topped with one fruit or another. You can use any dried fruit, reconstituted first in verjuice of course, or fresh apricots, blood plums, pears, quinces or apples that have been stewed, grilled or baked.

SERVES 8–10

---

200 g Australian dried apricots
¾ cup (180 ml) verjuice
120 g unsalted butter
150 g caster sugar
2 eggs
2 tablespoons brandy
finely grated zest of ½ lemon
2 tablespoons plain flour, plus extra for dusting
200 g ground almonds
1 quantity Sour-cream Pastry (see page 193)
cream, to serve

Soak the apricots in the verjuice overnight (or for at least several hours). Alternatively, place the apricots and the verjuice in a microwave-safe container and microwave on low for 2 minutes, then set aside for 20 minutes to reconstitute.

Using an electric mixer, beat the butter and sugar together until pale and creamy. Add one egg at a time, beating a little after adding each one to ensure that the mixture doesn't curdle. Add the brandy and lemon zest and mix to combine, then add the flour and ground almonds. Mix to combine well and set aside.

Drain the apricots and reserve any remaining verjuice.

Divide the sour-cream pastry in two, with one piece slightly larger than the other. Wrap both pieces in plastic film. Chill the larger piece in the refrigerator for at least 20 minutes and freeze the other piece for another use.

Grease a 22 cm × 4.5 cm tart tin with a removable base. Roll out the pastry on a lightly floured bench until 2–3 mm thick, then use to line the tart tin. Cut off the excess pastry around the edge, leaving 5 mm to allow for shrinkage as it cooks. Refrigerate for 20 minutes.

Preheat a fan-forced oven to 200°C (220°C).

Prick the pastry base with a fork, then line with foil, fill with pastry weights and blind bake for 15 minutes. Remove the foil and weights and bake for a further 5 minutes or until the pastry looks dry. Remove from the oven and leave for 10–15 minutes until cool.

Reduce the oven temperature to 175°C fan-forced (195°C).

Spread the almond mixture in the tart shell, then place the apricots, cut-side up, over the top and brush the surface with any reserved verjuice. Bake the tart for 30–40 minutes or until a toothpick inserted in the centre of the almond mixture comes out clean.

Serve the tart warm or at room temperature with a jug of cream alongside.

Verjuice and Golden Syrup Dumplings

Can golden syrup dumplings be improved upon? Well, if you love the idea of them but you don't really have a sweet tooth, these will appeal. The smell of these cooking is one of the more evocative aromas of my childhood. I've yet to find anyone (of my age, at least) who doesn't immediately get a smile on their face when I mention them. A jug of runny cream to serve is absolutely essential.

SERVES 4

1 cup (150 g) self-raising flour, plus extra for dusting
table salt
20 g unsalted butter
1 egg, beaten
50 ml milk
cream, to serve

SAUCE
1½ cups (525 g) golden syrup
½ cup (125 ml) verjuice
60 g unsalted butter

Preheat a fan-forced oven to 160°C (180°C).

Sift the flour and salt into a bowl, then rub in the butter with your fingers until the mixture resembles fine breadcrumbs. Add the egg and slowly stir in the milk until you have a firm dough, then set aside.

For the sauce, combine all the ingredients in an ovenproof saucepan with a tight-fitting lid. Bring to the boil over high heat, stirring to combine, then reduce the heat to low–medium and simmer until reduced and syrupy.

Meanwhile, lightly flour your hands and roll the dough into balls about 2.5 cm in diameter, placing them on a plate lined with baking paper as you go.

Slip the balls into the simmering syrup, then cover and transfer to the oven to cook for 10 minutes. Turn the dumplings and cook for a further 10 minutes or until they are puffed and cooked through.

Remove from the oven and allow the dumplings to rest in the sauce for 10 minutes. Transfer them to serving bowls with a slotted spoon, then serve with the sauce spooned over and a jug of cream to the side.

Verjuice and Extra Virgin Olive Oil Ice Cream

Don't let these ingredients frighten you. This ice cream has to be my favourite of all, as long as it's made with a young local extra virgin olive oil that has a light, grassy note. It feels like silk in the mouth, and the olive oil flavour shines without dominating the verjuice. It's the ice cream I wish I could make commercially, but I haven't yet been able to convince my marketing team it would sell, so here it is for you! It's wonderful served with any warm-from-the-oven fruit tart.

SERVES 4–6

200 g caster sugar
4 egg yolks
pinch of sea salt
finely grated zest of ½ lemon
200 ml extra virgin olive oil
200 ml verjuice

Combine the sugar with 100 ml water in a saucepan and heat over high heat for 1 minute or until dissolved and syrupy, then pour into a tray to cool the mixture quickly.

In an electric mixer, whisk the egg yolks, a pinch of salt and the lemon zest together to combine well. With the motor running, add the sugar syrup, then gradually pour in the olive oil in a thin, steady stream, whisking until incorporated. Gradually pour in the verjuice and whisk until incorporated. The mixture should have a smooth consistency, like a thin custard.

Transfer to an ice cream machine and churn for about 20 minutes according to the manufacturer's instructions, then freeze until firm.

BASICS

Verjuice Vinaigrette for Oysters

This dressing is amazingly fresh on the palate and I love to serve it spooned over freshly shucked oysters. I use my local South Australian pacific oysters, which are best from March to November. To keep unopened oysters fresh, wrap them in wet hessian or a wet tea towel when you get them home: they will keep this way for a couple of days. Open them just before eating for maximum flavour.

MAKES ¼ CUP (60 ML), ENOUGH FOR 12 OYSTERS

---

1 golden shallot, finely chopped
2 tablespoons verjuice
1 tablespoon extra virgin olive oil
1 tablespoon chervil (or micro herbs)
sea salt and freshly ground black pepper

Place the shallot and verjuice in a small bowl and leave for 15–20 minutes or until the shallot turns pink. Add the extra virgin olive oil, chervil or micro herbs and season to taste with salt and pepper.

Place all the ingredients in a jar with a screw-top lid, secure the lid and shake to combine.

Warm Verjuice and Poultry Jus Vinaigrette

The inspiration for this vinaigrette, which can be served warm with roasted or pan-fried chicken or drizzled over a warm chicken salad, comes from Steve Flamsteed, a very special member of the Pheasant Farm restaurant team. You can use the juices left over from roasting a chicken (or any poultry) – just measure out ¼ cup (60 ml) of the juices into a jar, leaving the fat behind, and add the verjuice and oil. Otherwise, a good homemade stock, reduced as described here, will do the job beautifully.

MAKES ABOUT 100 ML

---

1 cup (250 ml) Golden Chicken Stock (see page 190)
2 teaspoons verjuice
1½ tablespoons extra virgin olive oil
2 sprigs oregano or thyme, leaves picked
sea salt and freshly ground black pepper

Bring the chicken stock to the boil over high heat, then reduce the heat to medium and simmer for 10 minutes or until reduced to about 90 ml. Add the verjuice and continue to simmer for 5 minutes or until reduced to ¼ cup (60 ml). Remove from the heat and allow to cool a little. Transfer to a jar with a screw-top lid, add the extra virgin olive oil and herbs, then season. Secure the lid and shake to combine, then serve immediately.

Walnut Oil, Grape and Verjuice Vinaigrette

I make a fresh vinaigrette for every meal; this is the one I use with baby leaves. The ratio of oil to acidulant (in this case, verjuice) is different from the norm, but it really works here. Once opened, walnut oil keeps in the fridge for months.

MAKES ¾ CUP (180 ML)

⅓ cup (80 ml) verjuice
⅓ cup (80 ml) walnut oil
⅓ cup (60 g) green seedless grapes, halved
½ teaspoon Dijon mustard
sprig of lemon thyme, leaves picked
sea salt and freshly ground black pepper

Place all the ingredients in a jar with a screw-top lid, secure the lid and shake to combine.

 LEFT: Verjuice Vinaigrette for Oysters CENTRE: Warm Verjuice and Poultry Jus Vinaigrette RIGHT: Walnut Oil, Grape and Verjuice Vinaigrette

Golden Chicken Stock

One of the most important pieces of equipment in my kitchen would have to be the stockpot, though if you have a particularly large one, it's not always easy to find a home for it in your cupboards (even with the large country kitchen that I have, I need to keep mine in the shed!). There is something very satisfying about making your own stock; first taking the trouble to roast the bones and the vegetables, and then smelling it simmering away for hours with fresh herbs floating on the surface. I use verjuice rather than white wine when deglazing the bones, which gives a gentle acidity to the stock: otherwise I find it can be a little 'flat'. I like to make a large batch of stock and freeze it in 1 litre plastic takeaway containers to keep me going for the next 3 months. Remember to record the date on the container so your stash is always in good condition. This stock will keep for up to 4 days in the refrigerator.

MAKES ABOUT 3.5 LITRES

---

1 × 2.2 kg boiling chicken, cut into pieces (if you are using bones only, you will need 3 kg)
2 large onions, halved
1 large carrot, roughly chopped
extra virgin olive oil, for cooking
100 ml verjuice
1 large leek, trimmed, washed and roughly chopped
1 stick celery, roughly chopped
1 bay leaf
6 sprigs thyme
6 stalks flat-leaf parsley
1 head garlic, halved widthways

Preheat a fan-forced oven to 200°C (220°C).

Place the chicken, onion and carrot in a roasting pan and drizzle with a little olive oil. Roast for 20–25 minutes or until golden brown.

Transfer the chicken and vegetables to a large stockpot and place the roasting pan on the stove over high heat. Add the verjuice and simmer for 30 seconds or so, stirring and scraping the bottom of the pan, then tip the pan juices into the stockpot. Add the leek, celery, bay leaf, thyme, parsley and garlic to the stockpot, along with about 4 litres water; the chicken and vegetables should be covered. Bring to simmering point, then simmer uncovered for 3 hours.

Strain the stock immediately through a fine-meshed sieve into a bowl, then cool quickly by placing the bowl in a sink of cold water. Refrigerate or freeze until needed, removing any solidified fat from the surface before using.

Fish Stock

I tend to make a big pot of this stock, then freeze the leftovers to have on hand to create that last-minute sauce, risotto or soup where using a good fish stock will make all the difference. Frozen in an airtight container, this stock will keep for up to 3 months. In the fridge, it will keep for up to 4 days.

MAKES ABOUT 1.6 LITRES

1 kg snapper heads
20 g unsalted butter
½ large onion, diced
½ leek, diced
½ carrot, diced
½ stick celery, diced
2 button mushrooms, sliced
1 cup (250 ml) verjuice
6 stalks flat-leaf parsley
2 sprigs thyme
1 bay leaf
6 black peppercorns

Clean the snapper heads by cutting around the pointed underside of the head and the gills, then pull away the whole bottom part of the head and discard. Scrape out any traces of blood or innards, then rinse the heads carefully.

Melt the butter in a large stainless-steel stockpot over low–medium heat, then add the onion, leek, carrot, celery and mushroom and cook for 2 minutes, stirring occasionally to make sure they don't brown. Add the fish heads and cook for 1 minute. Increase the heat to high and pour in the verjuice. Bring to the boil and boil vigorously for 2 minutes. Pour in 2 litres water, then add the parsley, thyme, bay leaf and peppercorns. Bring to simmering point, then reduce heat to low and simmer for 20 minutes (don't allow the stock to boil at this stage as it will become cloudy).

Strain the stock immediately through a fine-meshed sieve into a bowl and set aside to cool, then refrigerate or freeze until needed.

Vegetable Stock

This is a great all-purpose stock that can be used in all kinds of soups, risottos and braises. You can vary the vegetables depending on what you have to hand. This stock will keep for up to 4 days in the fridge, or up to 3 months in the freezer.

MAKES ABOUT 1.3 LITRES

2 tablespoons extra virgin olive oil
1 large onion, quartered
1 clove garlic, roughly chopped
2 carrots, roughly chopped
2 sticks celery, roughly chopped
1 leek, white part only, trimmed, washed and roughly chopped
1½ tablespoons verjuice
50 g mushrooms, quartered
1 potato, roughly chopped
2 stalks flat-leaf parsley
1 sprig thyme

Heat the oil in a large stockpot over medium heat, then add the onion and cook for 8 minutes until golden brown. Add the garlic, carrot, celery and leek and cook for a further 4 minutes. Increase the heat to high and add the verjuice, stirring until it evaporates. Add the remaining ingredients and 2 litres water, then bring to the boil. Reduce to a gentle simmer and cook for 2 hours or until the stock has reduced by a third.

Strain the stock immediately through a fine-meshed sieve into a bowl and set aside to cool, then refrigerate or freeze until needed.

Salsa Agresto

You might see this as a pesto when you look at the ingredients, but the verjuice adds that 'brightness' or piquancy to the flavour (agresto is the Italian word for verjuice). This is best used straightaway, but will last for a couple of days in the fridge if quickly transferred to a jar and covered with a film of extra virgin olive oil to prevent oxidisation. Use it as you would pesto: dolloped onto bruschetta, spooned into soups, as a simple pasta sauce, or stirred through steamed vegetables.

MAKES 1 CUP (250 ML)

½ cup (80 g) raw almonds
½ cup (50 g) walnuts
2 large handfuls flat-leaf parsley leaves
handful basil leaves
1 clove garlic
sea salt and freshly ground black pepper
½ cup (125 ml) extra virgin olive oil
½ cup (125 ml) verjuice

Preheat a fan-forced oven to 200°C (220°C).

Place the almonds and walnuts on separate baking trays, then roast for 5 minutes or until golden, checking them frequently to make sure they don't burn.

Immediately wrap the roasted walnuts in a clean tea towel and then rub to remove the skins. Shake the walnuts in a sieve to get rid of the skins, then set aside with the almonds to cool.

Place the parsley, basil, garlic and ¾ teaspoon salt in a food processor with a dash of the olive oil, then add the cooled nuts and pulse until finely chopped. With the motor running, gradually add the oil in a thin, steady stream and blend until a paste forms. Season to taste with pepper, then pulse and add the verjuice at the last moment; the paste should be apple-green.

Serve immediately.

Bechamel Sauce

Bechamel sauce was only ever known as white sauce when I was growing up, and I learnt to make it at a very young age, judiciously adding the milk, then the stock, in stages so it wouldn't go lumpy. I used to dread Mum asking me to add parsley to the sauce, because I knew that meant we would be having it with tripe – the one food I detested as a child (I can assure you that's changed now, though!).

MAKES ABOUT 2 CUPS (500 ML)

40 g unsalted butter
¼ cup (35 g) plain flour
1 cup (250 ml) full-cream milk
1 cup (250 ml) Golden Chicken Stock (see page 190)
¼ cup (60 ml) verjuice
pinch of grated nutmeg
pinch of ground cinnamon
2 tablespoons finely grated Parmigiano Reggiano
sea salt and freshly ground black pepper

Melt the butter in a saucepan over medium heat, then remove from the heat and stir in the flour. Return the pan to the stove over low heat, stirring constantly with a wooden spoon for 3–4 minutes or until it turns very light golden (this is just to cook the flour, so it doesn't taste raw). Stirring continuously, pour in the milk and mix until incorporated. Gradually stir in the stock, adding ¼ cup (60 ml) at a time so the mixture doesn't become lumpy. Increase the heat to low–medium and bring to the boil, stirring continuously, then cook for 5 minutes or until the sauce starts to thicken (it should bubble gently). Stir in the verjuice; the sauce should now be thick enough to coat the back of a spoon. Stir in the nutmeg, cinnamon and Parmigiano and season to taste.

Verjuice Mayonnaise

This is such a delicate mayonnaise, more piquant and a little thinner than most, and yet it's the one I keep coming back to for its wonderful flavour. It's important to add the olive oil very slowly, drop by drop at first, until the mayonnaise starts to emulsify, at which point you can become a little bolder with your pouring. I've found that adding the extra virgin olive oil before the grapeseed oil helps to solidify the emulsion – don't ask me why, but it does. This mayonnaise will keep in the fridge for up to a week.

MAKES ABOUT 2 CUPS (500 ML)

---

2 egg yolks
⅓ cup (80 ml) verjuice
1 teaspoon finely grated lemon zest
½ teaspoon Dijon mustard
1 tablespoon chopped French tarragon
sea salt
¾ cup (180 ml) extra virgin olive oil
¾ cup (180 ml) grapeseed oil

Place the egg yolks, verjuice, lemon zest, mustard, tarragon and 1¼ teaspoons salt in a food processor or blender and blitz on high for 2 minutes. With the motor running, gradually pour in the olive oil, then the grapeseed oil in a slow steady stream until incorporated and thickened. Store in an airtight container and refrigerate until required.

Sour-cream Pastry

Sour-cream pastry is a stalwart of my cooking; I use it to make all variety of tarts and pies, both sweet and savoury. It's flaky and moreish, and I've never known it to fail. Here I've included just the steps for making the pastry itself – instructions on how to rest the pastry, roll it out and store any excess are given in the recipes on pages 78, 86, 178 and 182. It's good to know beforehand that the amount of sour cream needed can vary each time you make it, depending on the conditions. Start with about two-thirds of the sour cream at first, then add more as needed.

MAKES 575 G

1⅔ cups (250 g) plain flour, plus extra for dusting
200 g chilled unsalted butter, chopped
½ cup (120 g) sour cream

Process the flour and butter in a food processor until it resembles coarse breadcrumbs. With the motor running, gradually add about two-thirds of the sour cream at first, then add only enough of the remaining sour cream for the pastry to just come together to form a ball.

Turn out onto a lightly floured bench and bring the pastry together into a rectangle with your hands, then proceed as described in the relevant recipe.

ACKNOWLEDGEMENTS

This follow-up to my first book on verjuice has been a long time coming, and it would not have happened without the amazing Julie Gibbs, who is not only my publisher but a very special friend. She firmly believed it was time for another book on verjuice, to show people just how to use that bottle they'd snapped up in their enthusiasm but then were not quite sure what to do with.

As with every book I've done with Penguin, there's been such an amazing team of people to work with, that they begin to feel like family. My long-suffering editor, Virginia Birch, gently prodded me as needed yet never made me feel guilty, and was a delight to work with. She skilfully navigated the path between myself and the recipe tester Fiona Hammond, who cooked all the dishes to be sure they worked. What a journey that was! I learnt so much from Fiona, and I was so delighted when, at the end of the last day of testing, she said she was off to saute some wild mushrooms for dinner in – you guessed it – verjuice!

Daniel New is such a talent, and his design has once again astounded me. This is the third book of mine that Daniel has worked on, and each time he brings something so special and so different that I am in awe of his limitless imagination. I also have to thank him for generously lending props that belonged to his father for the photography.

Thanks also to the very special Kathleen Gandy, who came on board when there was still much to be sorted out; Megan Pigott, who coordinated the photoshoots so wonderfully well; and to production controllers Tracey Jarrett and Elena Cementon, for their hard work and tireless dedication to deadlines.

Thanks to the beautiful Sharyn Cairns, whose photographs, edgy and sophisticated yet still full of warmth, amazed me. I doubt we'll ever forget the three days of shooting in a severe heatwave, when we hired a huge cooling apparatus that failed entirely, but nothing upset her equilibrium. She is a true delight to work with. Thanks also to her assistants Saskia Wilson and Tess Kelly.

I would never have made my own verjuice way back in 1984 if it hadn't been for the belief that my friend, Peter Wall, had in the concept. And of all the winemakers I've worked with during every vintage since then, the one I most need to acknowledge is Trevor Jones, who, along with Lyn Tasker, is responsible for the technical side of the production of our verjuice. I've learnt so much from them.

A very special thanks to Janni Kyritsis and my great friend Stephanie Alexander who reinforced my belief in the potential of verjuice in those early days, when I would send them unlabelled flagons of the stuff to experiment with.

A huge thanks to Chris Wotton and Dianne Wooldridge, who worked tirelessly with me on each of the photoshoots, and to Cathy Radke and Julia Kretschmer, who helped to make sense of it on paper. And my everlasting thanks to my incredibly hard-working team at the Farmshop, past and present, who share their knowledge of verjuice with our visitors every day (with a special tip of the hat to Marieanne Pledger, who continually gets mentioned in dispatches . . .). Finally, a special thank you to Wayne Lyons, whose idea it was that every day at precisely 2 p.m., rain or shine, we would have that verjuice demonstration at the Farmshop. True brilliance!

INDEX

LANTERN

Published by the Penguin Group
Penguin Group (Australia)
707 Collins Street, Melbourne, Victoria 3008, Australia
(a division of Penguin Australia Pty Ltd)
Penguin Group (USA) Inc.
375 Hudson Street, New York, New York 10014, USA
Penguin Group (Canada)
90 Eglinton Avenue East, Suite 700, Toronto, Canada ON M4P 2Y3
(a division of Penguin Canada Books Inc.)
Penguin Books Ltd
80 Strand, London WC2R 0RL England
Penguin Ireland
25 St Stephen's Green, Dublin 2, Ireland
(a division of Penguin Books Ltd)
Penguin Books India Pvt Ltd
11 Community Centre, Panchsheel Park, New Delhi – 110 017, India
Penguin Group (NZ)
67 Apollo Drive, Rosedale, Auckland 0632, New Zealand
(a division of Penguin New Zealand Pty Ltd)
Penguin Books (South Africa) (Pty) Ltd
Rosebank Office Park, Block D, 181 Jan Smuts Avenue, Parktown North,
Johannesburg, 2196, South Africa
Penguin (Beijing) Ltd
7F, Tower B, Jiaming Center, 27 East Third Ring Road North, Chaoyang District,
Beijing 100020, China

Penguin Books Ltd, Registered Offices: 80 Strand, London, WC2R 0RL, England

First published by Penguin Group (Australia), 2012

10 9 8 7 6 5

Designed by Daniel New © Penguin Group (Australia)
Photography by Sharyn Cairns
Propping by Rachel Brown and Paul Hopper from York Productions
Typeset in Calluna and Alright Sans by Post Pre-press Group, Brisbane, Queensland
Colour reproduction by Splitting Image Colour Studio Pty Ltd, Clayton, Victoria
Printed and bound in China by 1010 Printing International Limited

National Library of Australia
Cataloguing-in-Publication data:

Beer, Maggie.
Maggie's verjuice cookbook / Maggie Beer.
9781921382628 (pbk.)
Includes index.
Grape products.
Cooking.

641.648

penguin.com.au/lantern

All the recipes in this book have been developed and tested using a fan-forced oven. If using a conventional oven, you'll generally need to increase the oven temperature by 20°C, as detailed in the recipes, but please note that cooking times may vary, depending on your individual oven.